This
BOOK
belongs to
Jamie
Love,
Robin
&
David

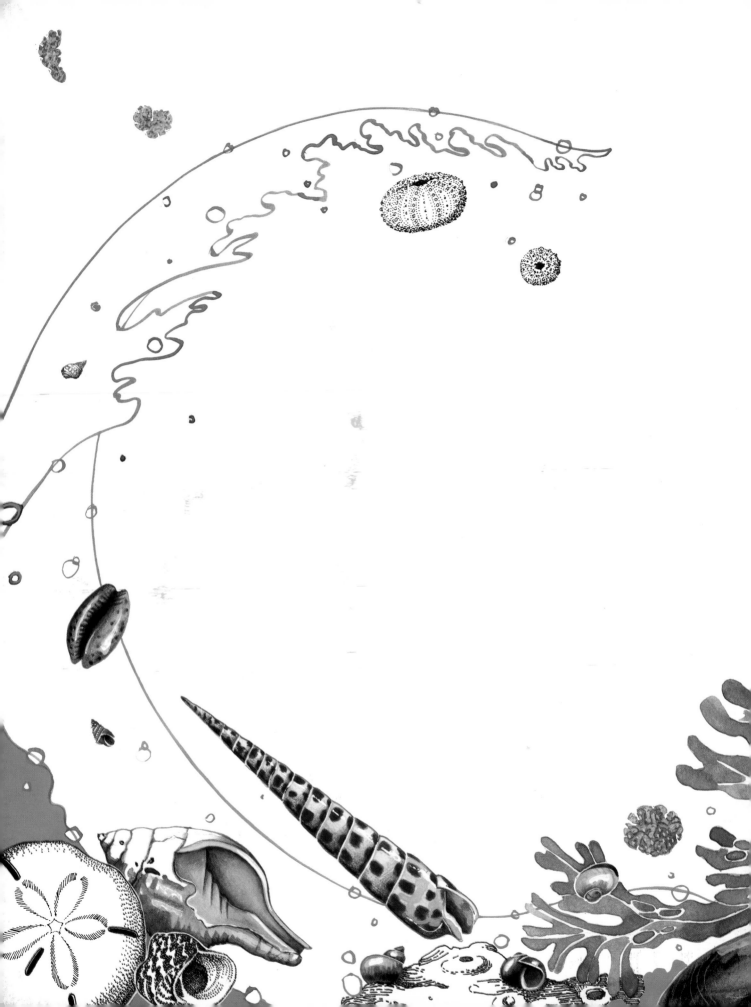

Neptune's GARDEN

SHELLS A to Z

WENDY FROST

A
BULFINCH
PRESS
BOOK

· LITTLE, BROWN *and* COMPANY ·
BOSTON · TORONTO · LONDON

·FIRST EDITION·

A
ROUNDTABLE PRESS
BOOK

Sweet
Ovalid

Shuttlecock
volva

LIBRARY of CONGRESS CATALOGING-IN-PUBLICATION DATA
FROST, WENDY.
   NEPTUNE'S GARDEN: SHELLS A to Z / WENDY FROST.—1ST. ED.
   P. CM.
   "A BULFINCH PRESS BOOK".
   ISBN 0-8212-1924-3
   1.SHELLS. 2.SHELLS-PICTORIAL WORKS. 3.SHELLCRAFT.
   4.SHELLS-FOLKLORE. 5.COOKERY(SHELLFISH) I. TITLE
   QL405. F76 1992
   594'.0471'.0222—DC20.   91-58379

The RECIPE for SUGAR REEF CONCH SALAD on page
20 is REPRINTED with PERMISSION of SUGAR REEF
RESTAURANT in NEW YORK CITY.
THE EXCERPT from "THE SHELL" on page 30 is
REPRINTED with PERMISSION from COLLECTED
POEMS of JAMES STEPHENS (New York:
Macmillan, 1954) and COURTESY of the Society
of Authors on behalf of the COPYRIGHT OWNER,
Mrs. IRIS WISE.
The EXCERPT from "THE CHAMBERED NAUTILUS"
on page 55 is REPRINTED from THE COMPLETE
POETICAL WORKS of OLIVER WENDELL HOLMES,
Cambridge Edition (Boston: Houghton Mifflin).

BULFINCH PRESS is an IMPRINT and TRADEMARK
of LITTLE, BROWN and COMPANY (Inc.)
PUBLISHED simultaneously in CANADA by
LITTLE, BROWN & COMPANY (Canada) LIMITED.

PRINTED IN SINGAPORE

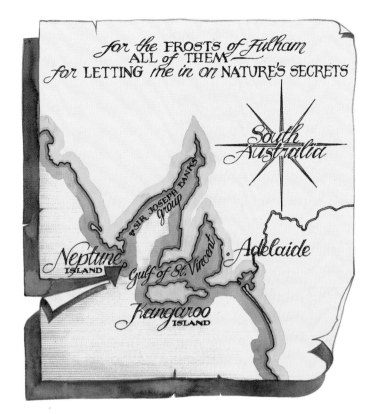

for the FROSTS of Fulham
ALL of THEM —
for LETTING me in on NATURE'S SECRETS

South
Australia

Sir Joseph Banks
group

Neptune
ISLAND

Gulf of St. Vincent

Adelaide

Kangaroo
ISLAND

I would like to thank
Marsha Melnick and Susan E. Meyer
at Roundtable Press,
and especially Sue Heinemann,
who made many an editorial "housecall."
Without their guidance
and expertise,
I would not be writing this acknowledgment.
My thanks also to Lindley Boegehold
at Bulfinch Press
for her advice and enthusiasm,
and to Paul Jones
for his gift of shells,
his friendship, and his counsel throughout.
I would also like to thank
Rosemary Drysdale
for her help with the needlepoint project
and Philip Reynolds, Dominick Anfuso, and
Joe Spieler for their advice
earlier on.
Finally, my thanks to Victor,
for keeping the home fires burning,
and
to my son,
D'Arcy Darwin,
with whom I've relived some of my tomboy days
collecting specimens for our museum.

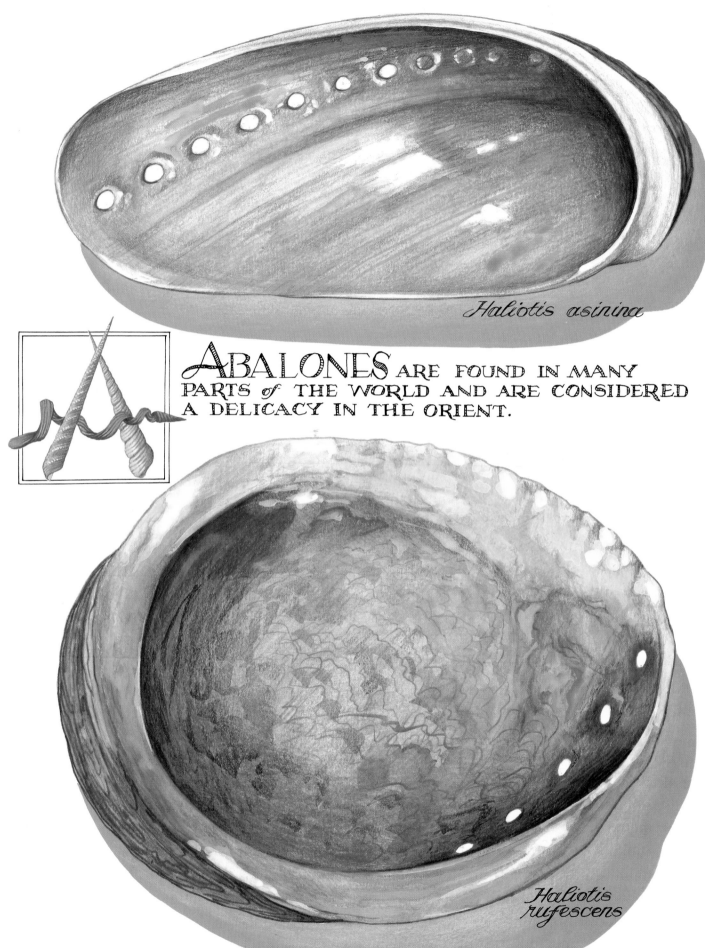

Haliotis asinina

ABALONES ARE FOUND IN MANY PARTS *of* THE WORLD AND ARE CONSIDERED A DELICACY IN THE ORIENT.

Haliotis rufescens

JAPANESE
SAKE
BOTTLE
LATE 19TH
CENTURY

THE MAORIS of NEW ZEALAND
COOKED ABALONE by FINELY
SLICING THE MEAT and HEATING
IT THROUGH BRIEFLY ON VERY
HOT STONES.

◆ABALONE◆
Before COOKING ABALONE
you MUST tenderize the meat.
CUT IT into SLICES and then
POUND with the flat side of
a WOODEN MALLET to
SOFTEN. The simplest way
to COOK ABALONE is to
SAUTÉ it in BUTTER for
NO MORE than a MINUTE
on EACH SIDE. Do not
OVERCOOK, or the MEAT
will BECOME TOUGH.
Serve with a SQUEEZE
of LEMON.

KOREAN
SILK SPOOLS

THE IRIDESCENT
MOTHER-of-PEARL
from the INSIDE of
ABALONE SHELLS
HAS BEEN USED FOR
CENTURIES AS DECORATIVE
INLAY on BOXES, FURNITURE,
and OTHER PRECIOUS OBJECTS.
SOME UNUSUAL APPLICATIONS INCLUDE A SAKE BOTTLE
MADE from TWO GOURDS, SILK SPOOLS FOUND IN THE
COLLECTION of the BRITISH MUSEUM, AND THESE
LARGE FISH HOOKS MADE BY NATIVES of the
SOUTH PACIFIC.

7

ARCHITECTONICA · SUNDIAL · PERFECT SPIRALS · NATURE'S ONE OF · WATERS · TROPICAL IN LIVES · MAXIMA · PERSPECTIVA NOBIUS ·

Gem Pimplet Anemone

Australian Pheasant Shell

FOUND ONLY ALONG
the SHORES *of*
SOUTHERN AUSTRALIA.
A FRAGILE, BEAUTIFULLY
MARKED CREATURE.
ONE *of the* MANY SHELLS
I COLLECTED AS A CHILD.

AS THEIR NAME IMPLIES
MOST SEA ANEMONES LOOK
MORE LIKE FLOWERS THAN POLYPS.
THEIR TENTACLES, USUALLY BRIGHTLY
COLORED, EXPAND LIKE FLOWER PETALS
TO TRAP LARVAE *of* SHRIMP, LOBSTER,
OR CRAB.

*Phasianella
australis*

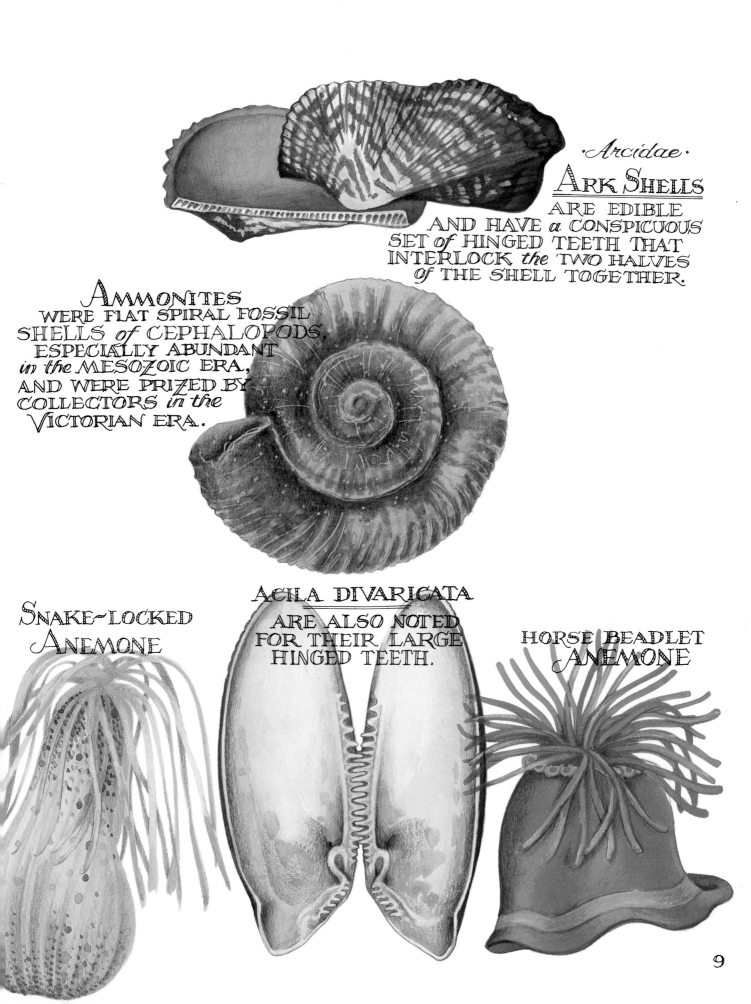

·Arcidae·

ARK SHELLS
ARE EDIBLE
AND HAVE a CONSPICUOUS
SET of HINGED TEETH THAT
INTERLOCK the TWO HALVES
of THE SHELL TOGETHER.

AMMONITES
WERE FLAT SPIRAL FOSSIL
SHELLS of CEPHALOPODS,
ESPECIALLY ABUNDANT
in the MESOZOIC ERA,
AND WERE PRIZED BY
COLLECTORS in the
VICTORIAN ERA.

SNAKE-LOCKED
ANEMONE

ACILA DIVARICATA
ARE ALSO NOTED
FOR THEIR LARGE
HINGED TEETH.

HORSE BEADLET
ANEMONE

9

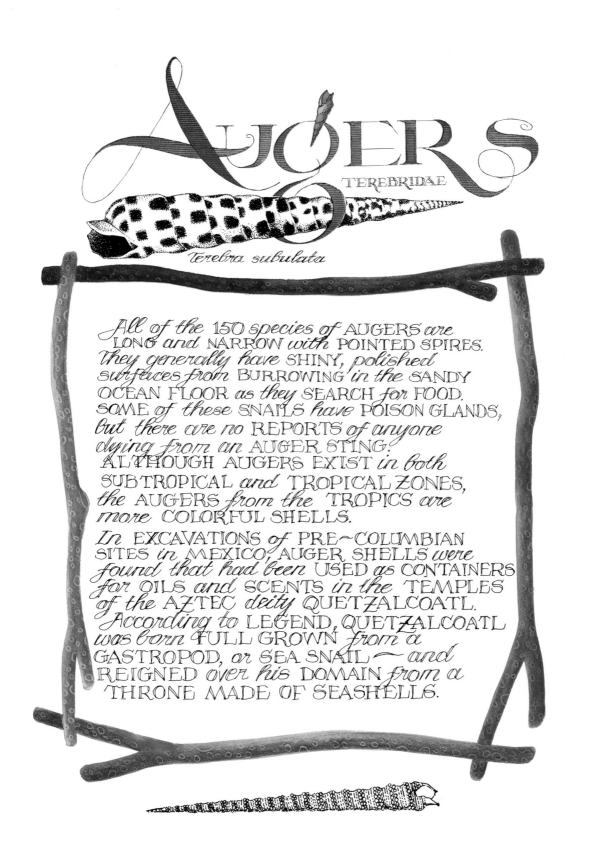

AUGERS
TEREBRIDAE

Terebra subulata

All of the 150 species of AUGERS are LONG and NARROW with POINTED SPIRES. They generally have SHINY, polished surfaces from BURROWING in the SANDY OCEAN FLOOR as they SEARCH for FOOD. SOME of these SNAILS have POISON GLANDS, but there are no REPORTS of anyone dying from an AUGER STING. ALTHOUGH AUGERS EXIST in both SUBTROPICAL and TROPICAL ZONES, the AUGERS from the TROPICS are more COLORFUL SHELLS.

In EXCAVATIONS of PRE~COLUMBIAN SITES in MEXICO, AUGER SHELLS were found that had been USED as CONTAINERS for OILS and SCENTS in the TEMPLES of the AZTEC deity QUETZALCOATL. According to LEGEND, QUETZALCOATL was born FULL GROWN from a GASTROPOD, or SEA SNAIL ~ and REIGNED over his DOMAIN from a THRONE MADE OF SEASHELLS.

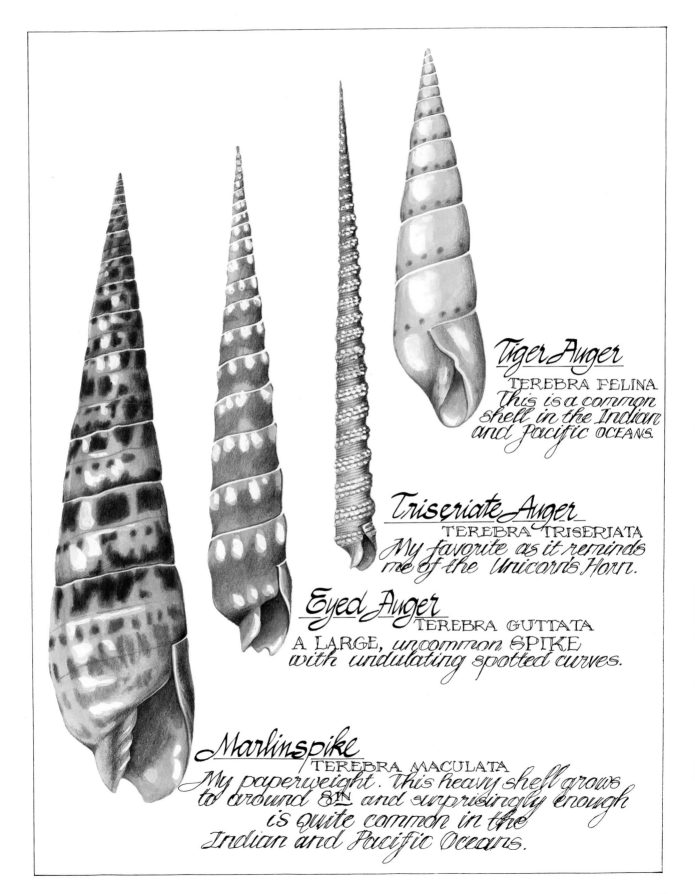

Tiger Auger
TEREBRA FELINA
This is a common
shell in the Indian
and Pacific OCEANS.

Triseriate Auger
TEREBRA TRISERIATA
My favorite as it reminds
me of the Unicorn's Horn.

Eyed Auger
TEREBRA GUTTATA
A LARGE, uncommon SPIKE
with undulating spotted curves.

Marlinspike
TEREBRA MACULATA
My paperweight. This heavy shell grows
to around 8IN and surprisingly enough
is quite common in the
Indian and Pacific Oceans.

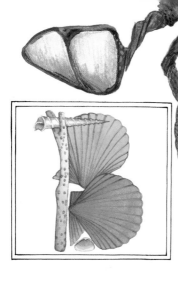

GOOSE BARNACLES
THEY ARE FOUND IN ALL SEAS CLINGING TO BOAT HULLS OR ANY FLOATING OBJECT.

BIVALVES ARE SHELLS
COMPOSED of TWO EQUAL PARTS HELD TOGETHER BY AN ELASTIC LIGAMENT. THEY are MOSTLY SEDENTARY ANIMALS LYING IN WAIT UNTIL THEIR FOOD FLOATS BY. THEY EAT PLANKTON AND MINUTE PIECES of ORGANIC MATTER.

The Channeled
BONNET
GROWS TO ABOUT 2 IN. LONG AND IS COLLECTED and ADMIRED for ITS DEEPLY CHANNELED GROOVES.

Phalium canaliculatum

The BRAIN CORAL SKELETON
IS MADE UP OF COLONIES OF SMALL CORAL POLYPS. COMMON IN THE TROPICS.

Atyidae

PAPER
BUBBLE SHELLS
SO CALLED *for their* FRAGILE, UNFURLED
STRIPED SHELLS.

BALER SHELLS
SOME SPECIES CAN GROW TO 14 IN. THEY HAVE
BEEN USED BY NATIVE PEOPLES AS COOKING
POTS, CONTAINERS, *and* WATER CARRIERS AS
WELL AS FOR BAILING
OUT WATER FROM
SHIPS *and* CANOES.

Melo amphora

13

GIANT CLAM
·:· Tridacnidae ·:·

CLAMS are BIVALVES. Although many of the SMALLER ONES are EATEN as FOOD, some of the LARGER, MORE DECORATIVE ONES HAVE BEEN USED SINCE ANCIENT TIMES in GARDENS and FOUNTAINS.

This BEAUTIFULLY CARVED and INCISED GIANT CLAM SHELL (10 IN. ACROSS) WAS USED as a COSMETIC CONTAINER by a FORTUNATE ETRUSCAN WOMAN and is now on DISPLAY in the BRITISH MUSEUM

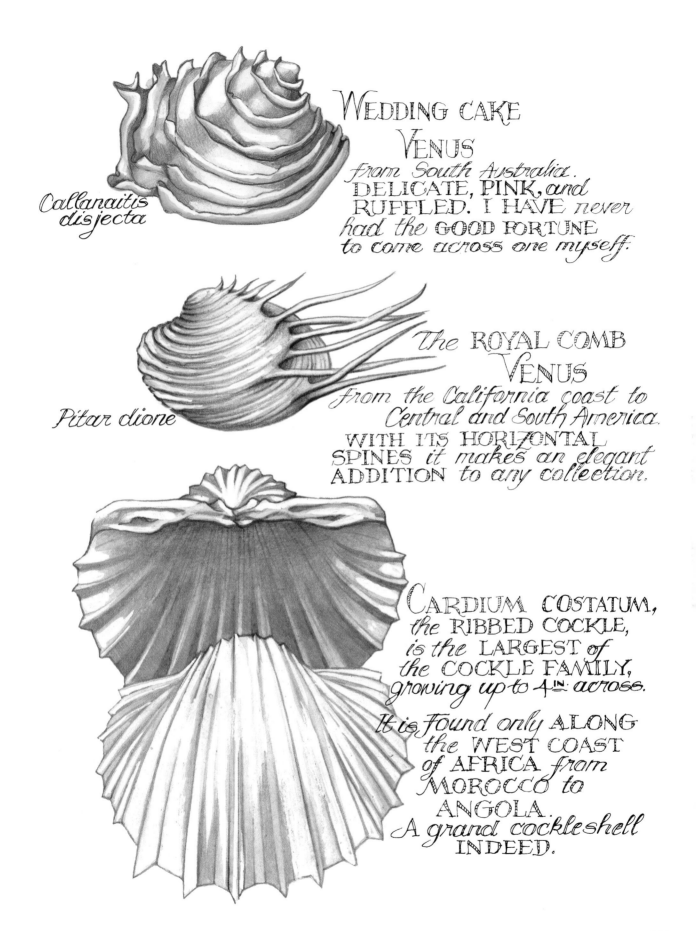

WEDDING CAKE
VENUS
from South Australia.
DELICATE, PINK, and
RUFFLED. I HAVE never
had the GOOD FORTUNE
to come across one myself.

Callanaitis
disjecta

The ROYAL COMB
VENUS
from the California coast to
Central and South America.
WITH ITS HORIZONTAL
SPINES it makes an elegant
ADDITION to any collection.

Pitar dione

CARDIUM COSTATUM,
the RIBBED COCKLE,
is the LARGEST of
the COCKLE FAMILY,
growing up to 4 IN. across.

It is found only ALONG
the WEST COAST
of AFRICA from
MOROCCO to
ANGOLA.
A grand cockleshell
INDEED.

the COCKLE
·Cardiidae·

THIS ANCIENT GREEK PERFUME BOTTLE *in the* BRITISH MUSEUM, *from the* 6TH CENTURY B.C., WAS MADE TO REPRESENT A COCKLESHELL.

LYRATE COCKLE · COSTATE COCKLE · HEART COCKLE   OBLONG COCKLE

HALF-HEART COCKLE

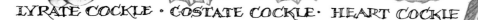

·CUTTLEFISH INK RISOTTO·

1 *medium* ONION, *finely chopped*
3 *tablespoons* BUTTER
2 *cups Arborio Italian* RICE
3 *cups chicken or vegetable* STOCK
1 *cup white* WINE
3 *medium-size* CUTTLEFISH
(*about 1 pound*), *thinly sliced.*
SACS *from* cuttlefish *or 1 packet* SQUID INK
2 *tablespoons* OLIVE OIL
½ *teaspoon* RED PEPPER FLAKES
salt and black pepper to taste
3 *tablespoons* PARMESAN *cheese*

In a heavy-based SAUCEPAN, SAUTÉ *the* ONION *until* CLEAR *in 2 tblspns.* BUTTER. ADD *the* RICE, *coating it with the* BUTTER, *and* STIR *over low heat.* ADD *a* LADLE *of the* HOT STOCK *to the* RICE MIXTURE, *then add a cup of* WINE.
   AFTER *it is* ABSORBED, *add another* LADLE *of* STOCK; *wait until it is* ABSORBED, *stirring occasionally, and* ADD *more* STOCK— *continuing* UNTIL *the* STOCK *is finished* (*about 20 minutes*). MEANWHILE, *remove the ink sacs from the* CUTTLEFISH, *place them in a* SIEVE, *and mash them with the back of a spoon to remove the* INK. WASH *the* CUTTLEFISH *thoroughly and* SLICE *it.* TOSS *it in the* OLIVE OIL *and* BROIL *for no more than 5 minutes.* REMOVE *the* RICE *mixture from the heat and* STIR *in the* RED PEPPER FLAKES, *salt, black pepper, remaining butter, and* PARMESAN *cheese. Then stir in the* BLACK CUTTLEFISH INK.
Serve the CUTTLEFISH *on top of the* BLACK RISOTTO. *serves* 6.
NOTE: This recipe also tastes good without the cuttlefish ink.

THERE ARE MANY USES FOR
COWRIE SHELLS
Cypraeidae

ENGLISH
NUTMEG GRATER
made from a
COWRIE
SHELL.

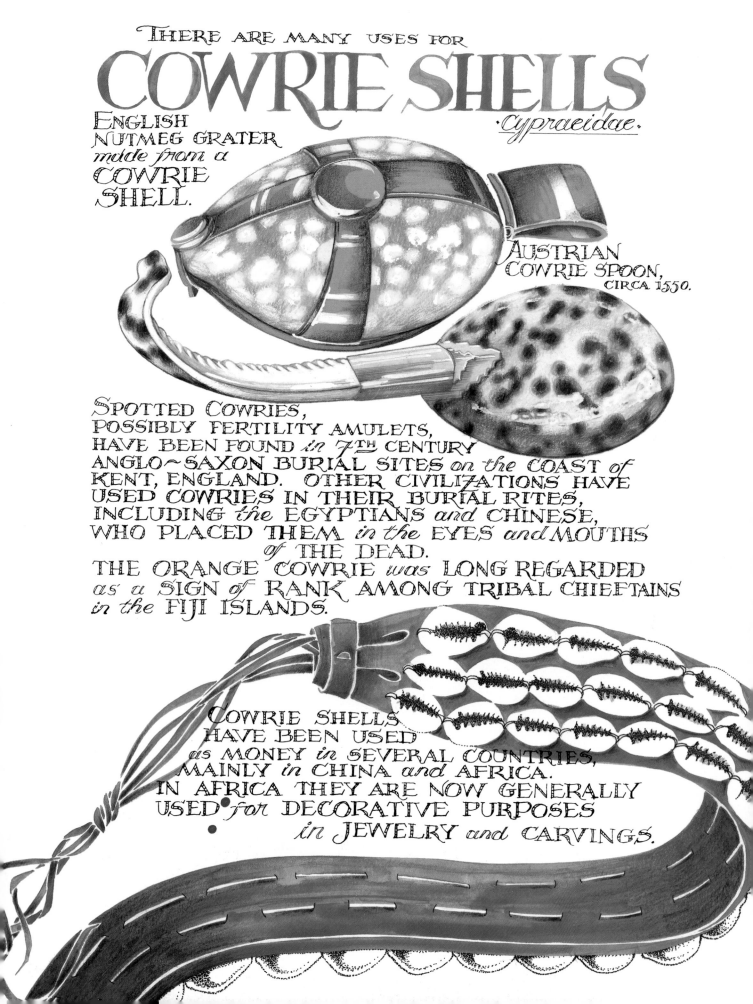

AUSTRIAN
COWRIE SPOON,
CIRCA 1550.

SPOTTED COWRIES,
POSSIBLY FERTILITY AMULETS,
HAVE BEEN FOUND *in* 7TH CENTURY
ANGLO~SAXON BURIAL SITES *on the* COAST *of*
KENT, ENGLAND. OTHER CIVILIZATIONS HAVE
USED COWRIES IN THEIR BURIAL RITES,
INCLUDING *the* EGYPTIANS *and* CHINESE,
WHO PLACED THEM *in the* EYES *and* MOUTHS
of THE DEAD.
THE ORANGE COWRIE *was* LONG REGARDED
as a SIGN *of* RANK AMONG TRIBAL CHIEFTAINS
in the FIJI ISLANDS.

COWRIE SHELLS
HAVE BEEN USED
as MONEY *in* SEVERAL COUNTRIES,
MAINLY *in* CHINA *and* AFRICA.
IN AFRICA THEY ARE NOW GENERALLY
USED *for* DECORATIVE PURPOSES
in JEWELRY *and* CARVINGS.

Cowries
CONTINUED

MY FRIEND and fellow artist PAUL JONES has a TIGER COWRIE that he BOUGHT in a JUNK SHOP in WALES. The SHELL had been SCRAPED BACK to the PURPLISH LAYER underneath the SPOTS and the LORD'S PRAYER had been ENGRAVED there by a VICTORIAN SAILOR at SEA.

Common Tiger Cowrie

This is a VERY RARE SHELL, one of only a few DOZEN KNOWN.

Spotted Cowrie

Fulton's Cowrie INHABITS DEEP WATER in and around SOUTH AFRICA. THIS RARE SHELL is almost ALWAYS FOUND in the STOMACHS of CERTAIN DEEP WATER FISH.

Fulton's Cowrie

Although NOT THE most BEAUTIFUL of COWRIES, Hirase's cowrie IS VERY RARE and BRINGS HIGH PRICES at AUCTION.

Hirase's Cowrie

This PRETTY PURPLISH COWRIE from the INDO~PACIFIC fades QUICKLY after IT IS COLLECTED.

Poraria Cowrie

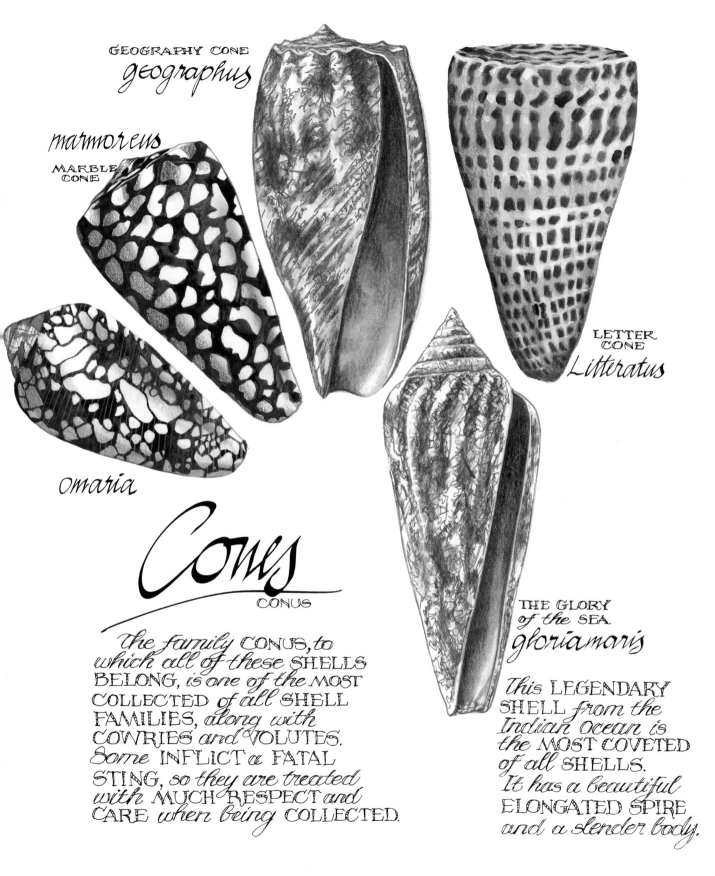

GEOGRAPHY CONE
geographus

marmoreus

MARBLE
CONE

omaria

LETTER
CONE
Litteratus

Cones
CONUS

The family CONUS, to
which all of these SHELLS
BELONG, is one of the MOST
COLLECTED of all SHELL
FAMILIES, along with
COWRIES and VOLUTES.
Some INFLICT a FATAL
STING, so they are treated
with MUCH RESPECT and
CARE when being COLLECTED.

THE GLORY
of the SEA
gloriamaris

This LEGENDARY
SHELL from the
Indian Ocean is
the MOST COVETED
of all SHELLS.
It has a beautiful
ELONGATED SPIRE
and a slender body.

19

SPIDER CONCH
Lambis Chiragra

A VEGETARIAN MOLLUSK
FOUND ONLY IN INDO~PACIFIC
WATERS. IT MOVES ABOUT
THE OCEAN FLOOR ON ITS
SPINY EXTENSIONS.

ROOSTER CONCH
Strombus gallus
SOMEWHAT
UNCOMMON.

Sugar Reef
CONCH *Salad*

1 *pound* CONCH MEAT, *diced*
1 *small* TOMATO, *diced*
1 CUCUMBER, *peeled and diced*
1 *small* RED ONION, *finely chopped*
¼ *cup* LIME JUICE (*about 2 limes*)
6 *tablespoons* ORANGE JUICE
1 *Scotch Bonnet* PEPPER, *seeded and finely chopped*
SALT *and* PEPPER *to taste*

POUND *the* CONCH MEAT *with a meat mallet for*
several MINUTES *to tenderize.* IN *a large* MIXING
BOWL, *combine all the* INGREDIENTS, *stir well, and*
COVER. REFRIGERATE *at least 2 hours to marinate*
the ingredients. SERVE COLD *as an* APPETIZER *or*
SIDE DISH. *Serves* 4~5.

QUEEN CONCH
Strombus gigas

THIS CARIBBEAN CONCH IS SOMETIMES
USED AS A TRUMPET HORN.
OCCASIONALLY A QUEEN CONCH PRODUCES
A BEAUTIFUL
PINK PEARL.

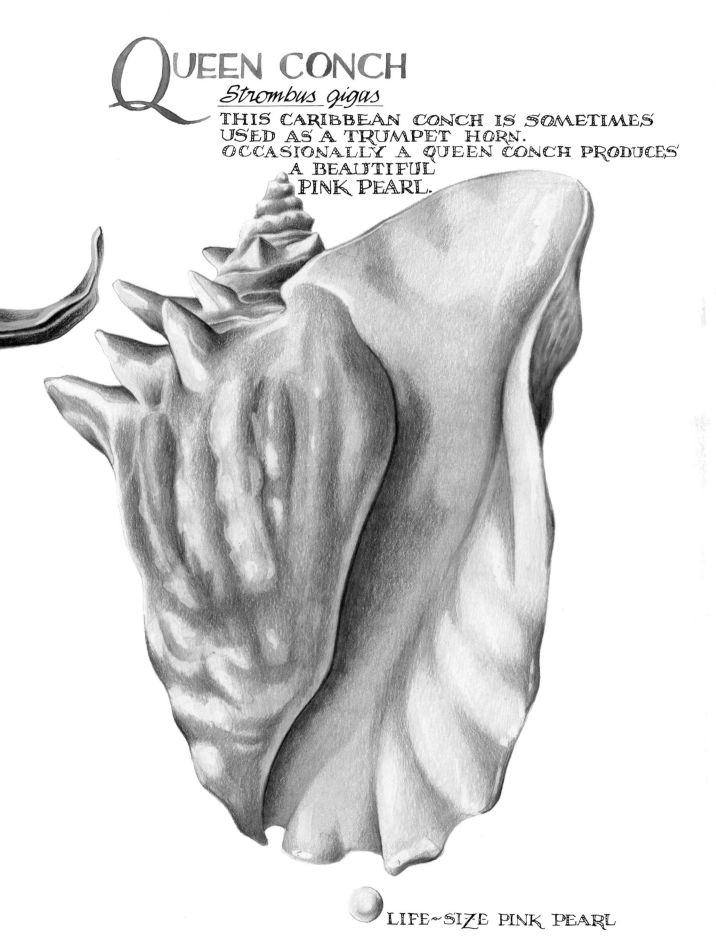

LIFE~SIZE PINK PEARL

21

DECATOPECTEN *plica*

or Folded Scallop

A MOTTLED SPECIMEN FOUND ONLY *in* SOUTHEAST ASIA.

VICTOR DAN'S
DELPHINULA
Angaria victani
FOUND *in the*
CORAL REEFS *of the*
PHILIPPINES

A JAPANESE
DELPHINULA

an INDO~PACIFIC
DELPHINULA

DRUPE SHELLS
ARE TINY COLORFUL CORAL
ROCK DWELLERS RELATED
to the COMMON DOG WINKLE

My UNCLE DOUG
CRUSHED
THIS TYPE *of*
DRILL SHELL
TO MAKE
"SHELL GRIT,"
COMMONLY
USED ON
PATHS *and*
DRIVEWAYS
in AUSTRALIA.
As A SMALL
CHILD, I USED
to RIDE *in the*
DUMP TRUCK
OUT TO THE
MANGROVE
SWAMPS
WHERE THE
SHELLS WERE
COLLECTED
and BROUGHT
BACK *to*
ADELAIDE
to be
GROUND DOWN.
THEY WERE
STOCKPILED
IN PEAKS
up to 25ft *high,*
WHICH PROVED
TO BE AN
IRRESISTIBLE
SLIDE.

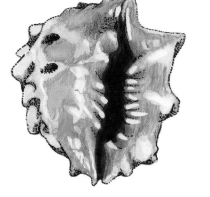

ECHINODERMS

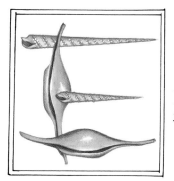

INCLUDE SEA URCHINS and SAND DOLLARS.

SINCE the DAYS of ANCIENT GREECE and ROME, SEA URCHINS HAVE BEEN SERVED as a MEDITERRANEAN DELICACY. THEY APPEAR in the FEASTS of MANY LEGENDS in GREEK MYTHOLOGY and are COMMONLY EATEN in JAPAN as SUSHI. THEY are BEST SERVED RAW on a BED of SEAWEED, CUT in HALF TO EXPOSE THEIR CORAL~COLORED FLESH. ADD a SQUEEZE of LEMON JUICE and SCOOP the FLESH OUT with a SLICE of GOOD CRUSTY BREAD. SEA URCHINS are ALSO USED in the CLASSIC BOUILLABAISSE. THEIR SALTY TASTE MAKES the SOUP more REDOLENT of the SEA.

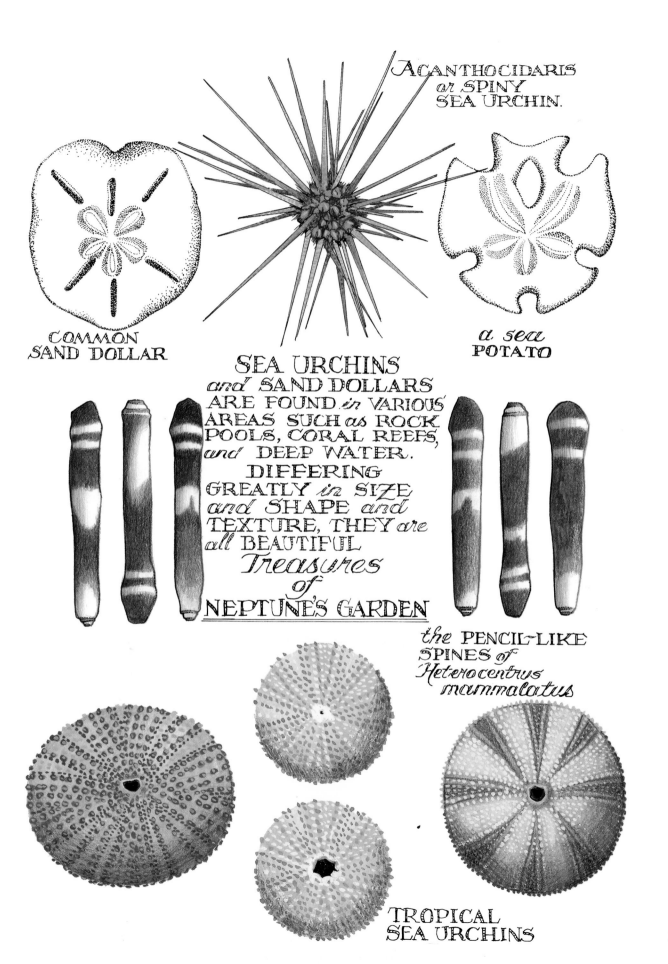

ACANTHOCIDARIS
or SPINY
SEA URCHIN.

COMMON
SAND DOLLAR

a sea
POTATO

SEA URCHINS
and SAND DOLLARS
ARE FOUND in VARIOUS
AREAS SUCH as ROCK
POOLS, CORAL REEFS,
and DEEP WATER.
DIFFERING
GREATLY in SIZE
and SHAPE and
TEXTURE, THEY are
all BEAUTIFUL
Treasures
of
NEPTUNE'S GARDEN

the PENCIL-LIKE
SPINES of
Heterocentrus
mammalatus

TROPICAL
SEA URCHINS

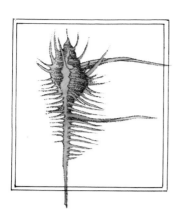

Fig shell

Ficidae.

A STREAMLINED, FRAGILE
LARGE SNAIL SHELL THAT FEEDS on
SAND DOLLARS and SEA URCHINS.
THE LIVING MOLLUSK is USUALLY
LARGER than the SHELL and almost
ENCASES IT, LEAVING only the BACK
EXPOSED.

FROG SHELLS
·Bursidae·

THE LARGER VARIETIES WERE ONCE USED as OIL LAMPS.

Fossil shells

THESE SPECIMENS were FOUND in 1989 by ME and my SON WHEN WE WERE CLIMBING a CLIFF by the MURRAY RIVER in SOUTH AUSTRALIA, SOME 200 miles or so INLAND. IT WAS VERY EXCITING to DIG OUT the OYSTERS and SAND DOLLARS THAT HAD BEEN BURIED EONS AGO WHEN THIS AREA was an INLAND SEA.

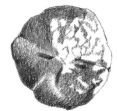

27

SEA~SHELL FRIEZE

MATERIALS: Acetate, very heavy vellum, or card stock · felt tip pen or pencil · craft knife · newspaper · masking tape · spray adhesive · 1 can each coral, aqua, and pale yellow water-based paint spray paint.

1. Trace the DESIGN onto the ACETATE, VELLUM, or CARDSTOCK with a PEN or PENCIL, leaving a BORDER of 3 INCHES on EACH SIDE. Then CUT OUT the STENCIL on a firm CUTTING SURFACE.

2. PLACE the STENCIL face down on a NEWSPAPER and SPRAY the BACK with ADHESIVE, making it tacky. USE proper VENTILATION.

3. FAINTLY RULE a STRAIGHT LINE on the SURFACE where you WANT the STENCIL. Place the STENCIL on this LINE and PRESS the EDGES DOWN lightly so PAINT won't SEEP underneath. USE MASKING TAPE around the EDGES. YOU CAN also USE CARDBOARD to MASK off AREAS around the STENCIL.

4. HOLD the YELLOW CAN 4~6 IN. AWAY and lightly SPRAY in a random pattern. Then LIGHTLY SPRAY the CORAL, then the AQUA, slightly OVERLAPPING for a MOTTLED EFFECT.

5. LINE UP the DESIGN and REPEAT as DESIRED.

And then I pressed the shell
close to my ear
and listened well,
and straightway like a bell
came low and clear
the slow, sad murmur
of the distant seas,
whipped by an icy breeze
upon a shore
windswept and desolate.

James Stephens

GLOBULARIA
fluctuata
·NATICACEA·

A thick, smooth, VERY
ROUND SHELL *with just*
a SMALL SWIRL *at the*
top. This carnivore is
FAMOUS *for making* HOLES
in its VICTIMS' SHELLS
It is generally found in WARM
SANDY BAYS.

the GUILDFORDIA YOKA

GROWS SPINES *so*
as to PROTECT ITSELF
from BEING TURNED
OVER *and* HAVING ITS
EDIBLE BODY EXPOSED
to PREDATORS.

SUPERB GAZA
this BEAUTIFUL
IRIDESCENT SHELL
is found in
DEEP WATER
off the COAST
of MEXICO.

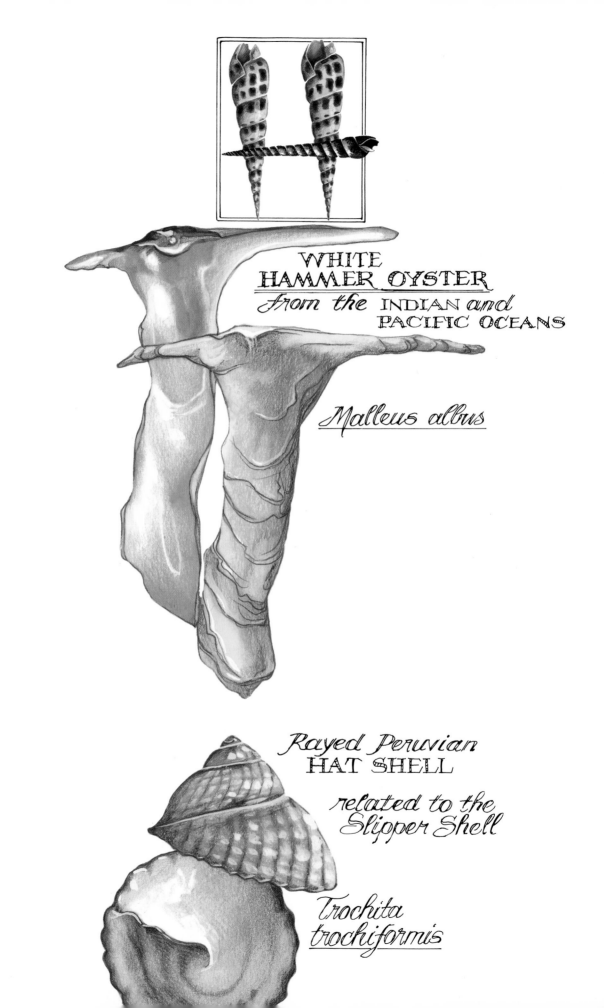

WHITE
HAMMER OYSTER
from the INDIAN and
PACIFIC OCEANS

Malleus albus

Rayed Peruvian
HAT SHELL

related to the
Slipper Shell

Trochita
trochiformis

Harp
SHELL

THIS SNAIL LIVES
BURIED *in the* SAND
and FEEDS *on* CRABS,
SHRIMP, *and* SEA
URCHINS THAT IT
CAPTURES *by* ENVELOPING
and SMOTHERING THEM
with its "FOOT." IT CAN ALSO
MAKE *a* QUICK ESCAPE *from*
PREDATORS
by
LOSING *the*
END *of its* FOOT.

*Pleuroploca
gigantea*

HORSE CONCH

THIS SHELL *is the*
LARGEST CARNIVOROUS
GASTROPOD *in the*
SOUTHERN UNITED STATES
and the CARIBBEAN.
IT *can* GROW *to* 20 inches.

BULL MOUTH
HELMET
Cypraecassis rufa

IN PROFILE, *as in the* DRAWING BELOW, *the* BULL MOUTH HELMET RESEMBLES *a* ROMAN GLADIATOR'S HEADDRESS. *This* HEAVY SHELL *has been* used by ARTISANS *for* CENTURIES *as a* MAIN SOURCE *for* CAMEOS.

ISOGNOMON ALATUS

THIS COMMON FLAT TREE OYSTER LIVES *in the* LOWER BRANCHES *of* MANGROVES.

ISOGNOMON ISOGNOMON

THIS COMMON SHALLOW-WATER OYSTER USES ITS EXTREMITIES *to* ANCHOR ITSELF *in the* SANDY BOTTOM *so that* IT CAN NOT *be* TURNED OVER *by* PREDATORS.

IMBRICARIA

punctata   conularis   olivaeformis

INDIAN CHANK

Turbinella pyrum

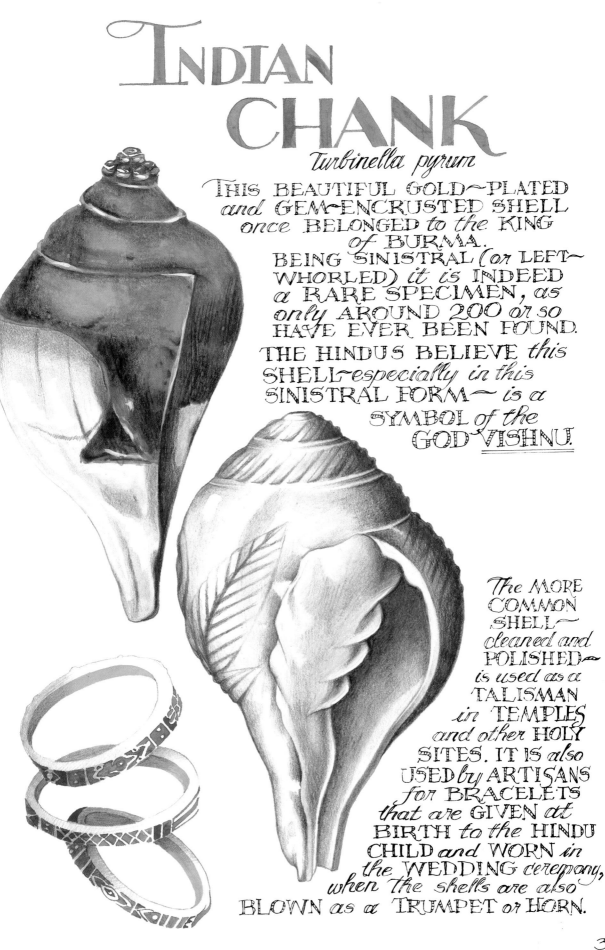

THIS BEAUTIFUL GOLD~PLATED and GEM~ENCRUSTED SHELL once BELONGED to the KING of BURMA. BEING SINISTRAL (or LEFT~WHORLED) it is INDEED a RARE SPECIMEN, as only AROUND 200 or so HAVE EVER BEEN FOUND. THE HINDUS BELIEVE this SHELL~especially in this SINISTRAL FORM~ is a SYMBOL of the GOD VISHNU.

The MORE COMMON SHELL~ cleaned and POLISHED~ is used as a TALISMAN in TEMPLES and other HOLY SITES. IT IS also USED by ARTISANS for BRACELETS that are GIVEN at BIRTH to the HINDU CHILD and WORN in the WEDDING ceremony, when the shells are also BLOWN as a TRUMPET or HORN.

JANTHINA

THESE THIN~ SHELLED VIOLET SEA SNAILS FLOAT ABOUT on the WATER SURFACE. WHEN PROVOKED they SQUIRT a PURPLE LIQUID, which ALLOWS them to ESCAPE.

JEWEL BOX SHELLS. Chamidae.

THESE BRILLIANTLY COLORED SHELLS ATTACH THEMSELVES to CORALS, ROCKS, or WRECKS. THEY BECOME HEAVILY ENCRUSTED with other FORMS of MARINE LIFE.

Lazarus Jewel Box

Leafy Jewel Box

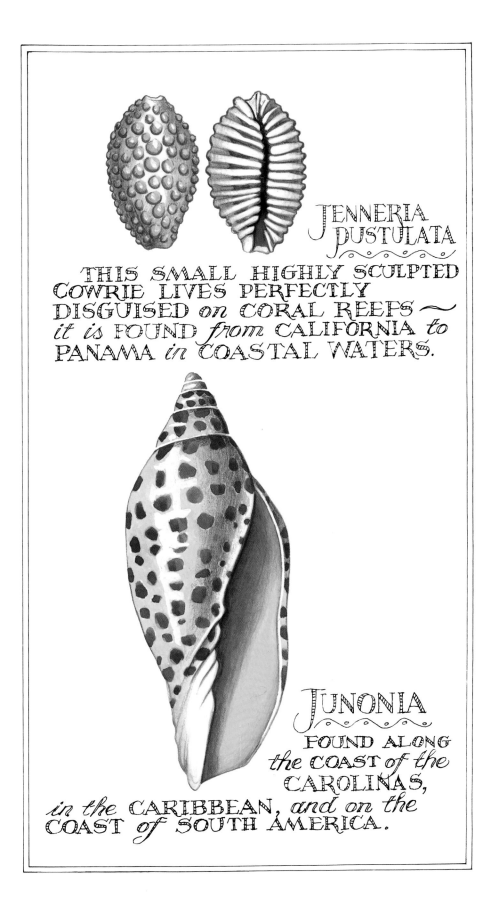

JENNERIA PUSTULATA

THIS SMALL HIGHLY SCULPTED COWRIE LIVES PERFECTLY DISGUISED on CORAL REEFS ~ it is FOUND from CALIFORNIA to PANAMA in COASTAL WATERS.

JUNONIA

FOUND ALONG the COAST of the CAROLINAS, in the CARIBBEAN, and on the COAST of SOUTH AMERICA.

39

JINGLE SHELL WIND CHIME·

WITH A JEWELRY BIT, DRILL HOLES *in the tops of* 8 *to* 10 SEA URCHIN SPINES *and in* ABOUT 18 SADDLE JINGLE SHELLS *(Placuna sella).* USING LINEN BUTTONHOLE THREAD, *hang the* SHELLS *from* 6 ¹ᴺᶜᴴ *and* 3¹ᴺᶜᴴ WIRE RINGS *(available at craft supply stores)* AS SHOWN IN THE DRAWING.

JINGLE JANGLE JINGLE JANGLE ♪ ♪ ♪♪

TINKLE ~ TINKLE

WIND CHIMES RESONATING *with*

TINKLE ~ TINKLE ~ MUSIC *of* LAZY

MAKE ONE TO REMIND YOU *of*

the WAVES BREAKING *as the*

Days of BEACHCOMBING

SOUND *of the* SEASHORE

JEWELED SEASHELL ·SCARF·

SELECT 40 to 50 TINY SHELLS *that you have* COLLECTED *at the* SEASHORE *and* DRILL HOLES *in them with a* JEWELRY BIT. *Take an* AQUA *or* SEA~GREEN PIECE *of* COTTON CHIFFON *and* CUT OUT *a* 36 INCH SQUARE. HEM *the* FABRIC *and* SEW *the* SHELLS AROUND *the* EDGES *at* RANDOM, *using the* FOUR LARGEST *at the* CORNERS.

The world is too much with us.

THE WORLD IS TOO MUCH WITH US; LATE AND SOON,
GETTING AND SPENDING, WE LAY WASTE OUR POWERS:
LITTLE WE SEE IN NATURE THAT IS OURS;
WE HAVE GIVEN OUR HEARTS AWAY, A SORDID BOON!
THIS SEA THAT BARES HER BOSOM TO THE MOON;
THE WINDS THAT WILL BE HOWLING AT ALL HOURS,
AND ARE UP-GATHERED NOW LIKE SLEEPING FLOWERS;
FOR THIS, FOR EVERYTHING, WE ARE OUT OF TUNE;
IT MOVES US NOT.—GREAT GOD! I'D RATHER BE
A PAGAN SUCKLED IN A CREED OUTWORN;
SO MIGHT I, STANDING ON THIS PLEASANT LEA,
HAVE GLIMPSES THAT WOULD MAKE ME LESS FORLORN;
HAVE SIGHT OF PROTEUS RISING FROM THE SEA;
OR HEAR OLD TRITON BLOW HIS WREATHED HORN.

William Wordsworth

KEYHOLE LIMPETS

are VEGETARIANS THAT LIVE *in* WARM *shallow* WATER. As *with the* ABALONE *and the* SLIT SHELL, *the hole in the top of the shell is used to* EXPEL WASTE PRODUCTS.

Fissurellidae

43

LIMPETS ACMAEIDAE

Latiaxis

MANY VARIETIES of LATIAXIS are FOUND in and AROUND JAPAN. IT IS FITTING THAT the DELICATE SHAPES of these SHELLS RESEMBLE PAGODAS and other FEATURES of JAPANESE DESIGN.

·MAGILIDAE·

The CARIBBEAN CORAL SNAIL makes its home in the base of LACE or FAN CORAL and EXTENDS ITSELF as the CORAL GROWS. IT BECOMES SO ENMESHED with the CORAL that it is UNABLE to FREE ITSELF. BUT THIS IS A PERFECT WAY to PROTECT ITSELF from PREDATORS.

The MAGILUS SNAIL

LIVES IN BRAIN CORAL in the INDO~PACIFIC. IT STARTS as a small WHITE SNAIL and GROWS a "TAIL" of WHORLS of SHELL MATERIAL.

·Mitridae·
MITERS

A BEAUTIFUL SPECIES *of* CARNIVOROUS
MOLLUSKS. THEY SCAVENGE *in all the*
WARM SHALLOW WATERS *of the* WORLD.
THEY *are* FOUND BURIED *in the* SAND,
GENERALLY UNDER ROCKS *and* CORALS.

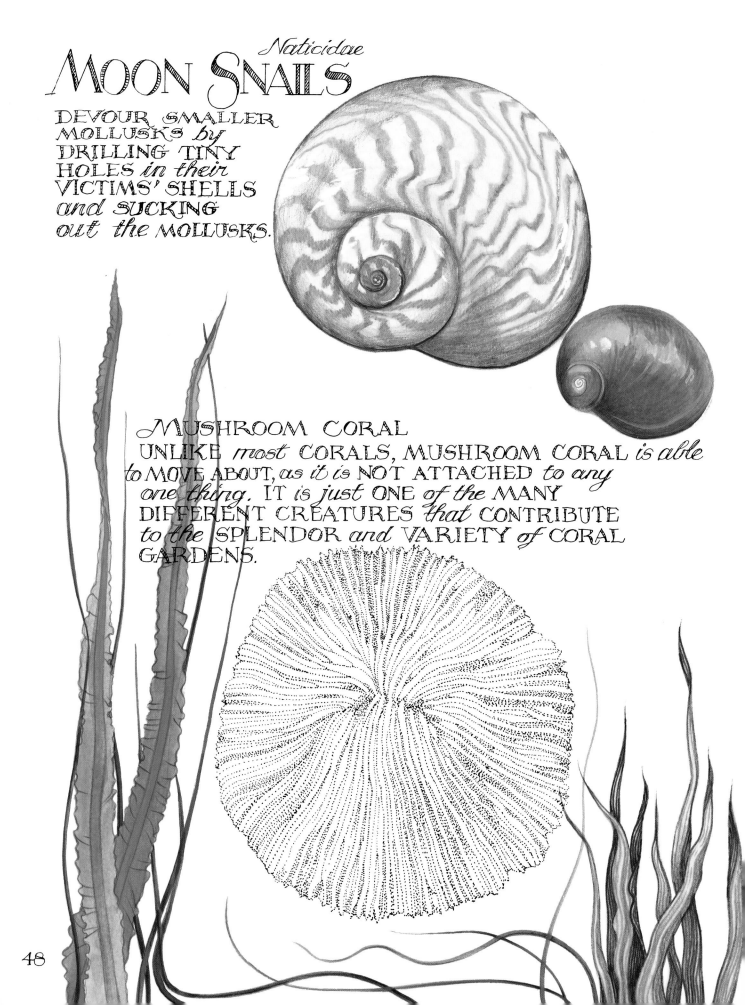

MOON SNAILS

Naticidae

DEVOUR SMALLER MOLLUSKS *by* DRILLING TINY HOLES *in their* VICTIMS' SHELLS *and* SUCKING *out* the MOLLUSKS.

MUSHROOM CORAL

UNLIKE *most* CORALS, MUSHROOM CORAL *is able* to MOVE ABOUT, *as it is* NOT ATTACHED *to any one thing.* IT *is just* ONE *of the* MANY DIFFERENT CREATURES *that* CONTRIBUTE *to the* SPLENDOR *and* VARIETY *of* CORAL GARDENS.

MUREX
SHELLS

THE PHOENICIANS
DISCOVERED *the*
SECRET *of* MAKING
PURPLE DYE *from*
Bolinus brandaris
and Hexaplex
trunculus.
THEY TRAVELED
far SEARCHING *for*
NEW BEDS *of* MUREX
SHELLS *as* MIDDENS
UNEARTHED *in* MALTA,
CARTHAGE, CADIZ, *and*
UTICA *have* PROVED.
THE PROCESS *used to*
EXTRACT *the* DYE
involved CRUSHING *and*
BOILING *the* SNAIL, *and*
the COLOR VARIED *from*
CRIMSON *to* VIOLET.
The ROMAN
EMPERORS DECREED
that they ALONE *were*
to have THE PRIVILEGE
of WEARING PURPLE.
AFTER *the* FALL *of the*
ROMAN EMPIRE, PURPLE
BECAME *an* OFFICIAL
COLOR *of the* CATHOLIC
CHURCH *and also of the*
BRITISH ROYAL FAMILY.

49

MUSSELS

SHELL MIDDENS are MOUNDS of EARTH FORMED when COASTAL TRIBES threw AWAY the SHELLS from their FEASTS and LEFT THEM to PILE UP at a SPOT NEAR THEIR ENCAMPMENT. MANY a MUSSEL SHELL MIDDEN has been EXCAVATED by ANTHROPOLOGISTS to give a CLEAR PICTURE of the DIET of other CIVILIZATIONS. OUR FAMILIAR BLUE MUSSEL, USED in the RECIPE on the page opposite, MAKES a perfect UTENSIL in itself FOR EATING OTHER MUSSELS.

ie. WHEN EATING MUSSELS, TAKE a FORK to REMOVE the FIRST MORSEL, THEN USING the "PERFECT PINCER" a SHELL that is STILL hinged together ~ PLUCK the OTHER JUICY MORSELS from their shells.

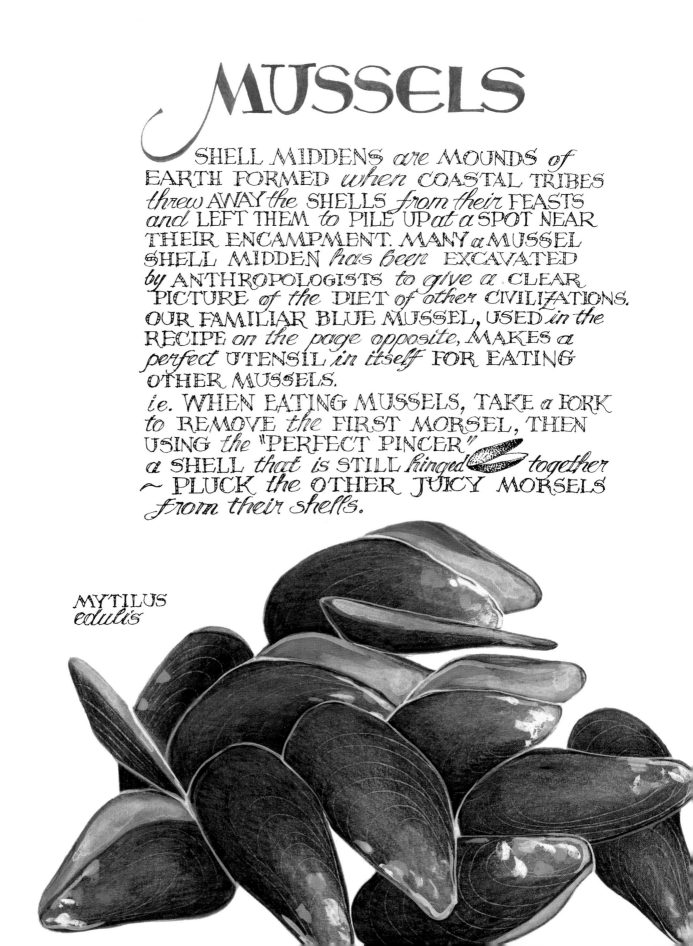

MYTILUS
edulis

MOULES

is FRENCH *for* MUSSELS, *which are the national dish of* BELGIUM.

◆ MUSSEL TAPAS ◆ *Tapas de Mejillones*

3 SPRIGS PARSLEY
1 CLOVE GARLIC
4 *tablespoons* BUTTER
3/4 *cup* GROUND ALMONDS
1/4 *teaspoon* RED PEPPER *flakes*
Pinch of SAFFRON THREADS
salt and pepper to taste
1 SLICE *white* BREAD, *soaked in* 1/4 *cup white* WINE
1 *tablespoon* WATER
4 *pounds* MUSSELS, *scrubbed and debearded*

Preheat the oven to 400°F. *Then make the* PICADA *(mixture).*
IN *a small* BOWL POUND TOGETHER *the* PARSLEY
and GARLIC, *then* MIX *in the* BUTTER. ADD *the*
ALMONDS, RED PEPPER FLAKES, SAFFRON *threads,*
salt, and pepper. SQUEEZE *the* EXCESS LIQUID *from*
the BREAD, ADD *it to the* MIXTURE, *and* WORK
everything into a PASTE.
IN *a tablespoon of* WATER, *steam open the* MUSSELS
over high heat —about 1 *or* 2 *minutes.* REMOVE *the*
TOP SHELL *of the* MUSSELS *and place them on an*
OVENPROOF PLATTER. SPOON 1 *teaspoon of the picada*
over EACH MUSSEL *and* BAKE *for* 6 *to* 7 *minutes.*
SERVE *immediately with a* BOWL *of* BLACK OLIVES,
peeled ROASTED ALMONDS, *and* CRUSTY BREAD.
SERVES 4.

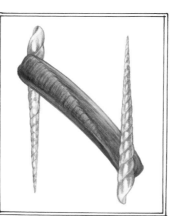

NEPTUNE

NEPTUNE, or NEPTUNUS in LATIN, WAS ORIGINALLY the GOD of ALL WATER in ANCIENT ROMAN MYTHOLOGY. THEN the ROMANS BEGAN to IDENTIFY HIM with the earlier GREEK GOD POSEIDON, so he became KNOWN as the GOD of the SEA. ANOTHER WISE OLD MAN of the MEDITERRANEAN was NEREUS, an ANCIENT GREEK SEA GOD and FATHER of the WATER NYMPHS. HE was usually DEPICTED with SEAWEED instead of HAIR on his HEAD, FACE, and CHEST.

IN 1965, on my FIRST VOYAGE out of AUSTRALIA, the CREW of the GREEK SHIP that I traveled on PERFORMED a RITUAL when we CROSSED the EQUATOR. KING NEPTUNE was brought on board, we were DOUSED with SEAWEED~LIKE STRANDS of SPAGHETTI, and many other PRANKS ENSUED, initiating us into the NORTHERN HEMISPHERE.

NEPTUNEA DECEMCOSTATA

The NEW ENGLAND

NEPTUNE SHELL

found along the coastline CANADA *to* MASSACHUSETTS

LABRADOR

QUÉBEC

NEWFOUNDLAND

·CANADA·

NOVA SCOTIA

Halifax

MAINE

Portland

MASS.

Boston

ATLANTIC OCEAN

·UNITED STATES of AMERICA·

New York

·*Philadelphia*

NAUTILUS
pompilius

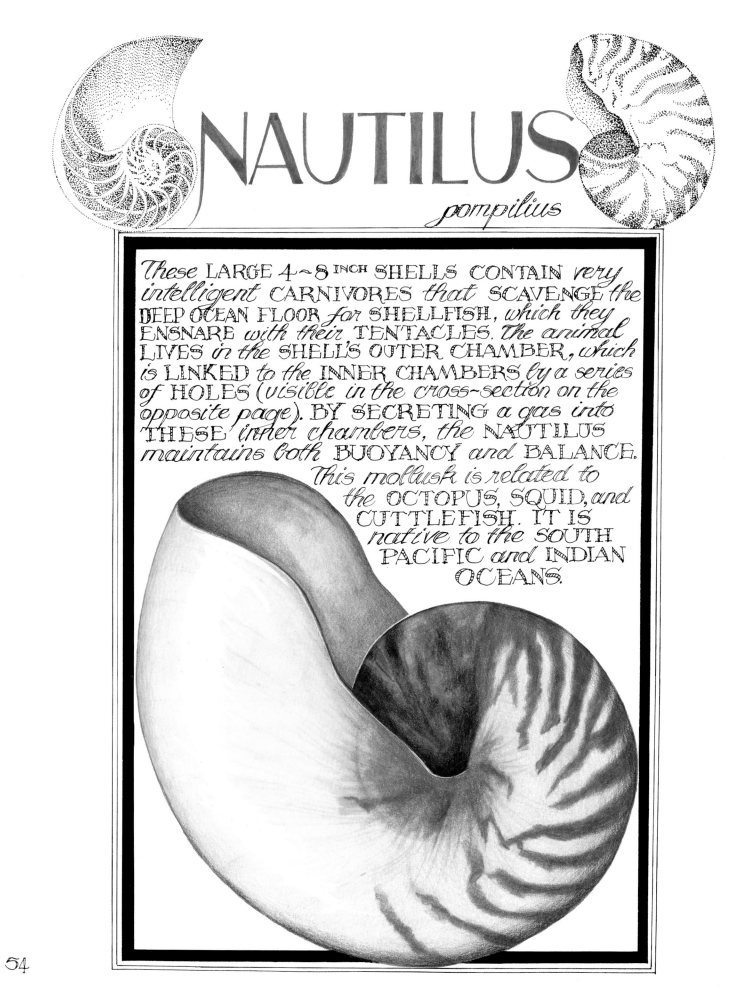

These LARGE 4~8 INCH SHELLS CONTAIN *very intelligent* CARNIVORES *that* SCAVENGE *the* DEEP OCEAN FLOOR *for* SHELLFISH, *which they* ENSNARE *with their* TENTACLES. *The animal* LIVES *in the* SHELL'S OUTER CHAMBER, *which* is LINKED *to the* INNER CHAMBERS *by a series* of HOLES (*visible in the cross~section on the opposite page*). BY SECRETING *a gas into* THESE *inner chambers, the* NAUTILUS *maintains both* BUOYANCY *and* BALANCE.

This mollusk is related to the OCTOPUS, SQUID, *and* CUTTLEFISH. IT IS *native to the* SOUTH PACIFIC *and* INDIAN OCEANS.

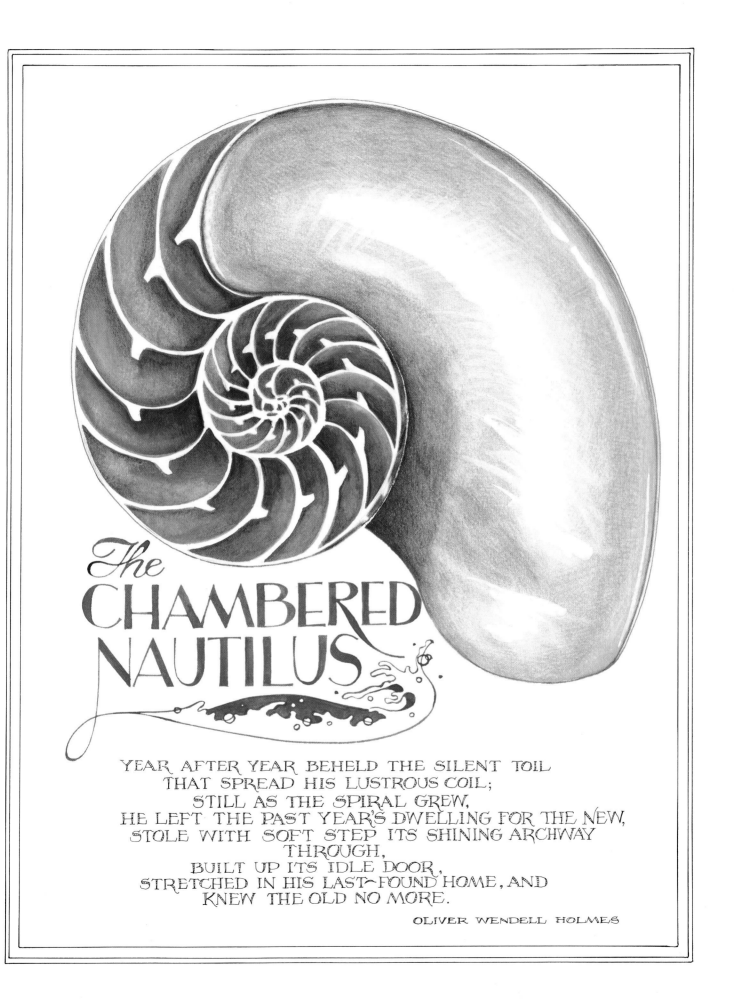

The CHAMBERED NAUTILUS

YEAR AFTER YEAR BEHELD THE SILENT TOIL
THAT SPREAD HIS LUSTROUS COIL;
STILL AS THE SPIRAL GREW,
HE LEFT THE PAST YEAR'S DWELLING FOR THE NEW,
STOLE WITH SOFT STEP ITS SHINING ARCHWAY
THROUGH,
BUILT UP ITS IDLE DOOR,
STRETCHED IN HIS LAST-FOUND HOME, AND
KNEW THE OLD NO MORE.

OLIVER WENDELL HOLMES

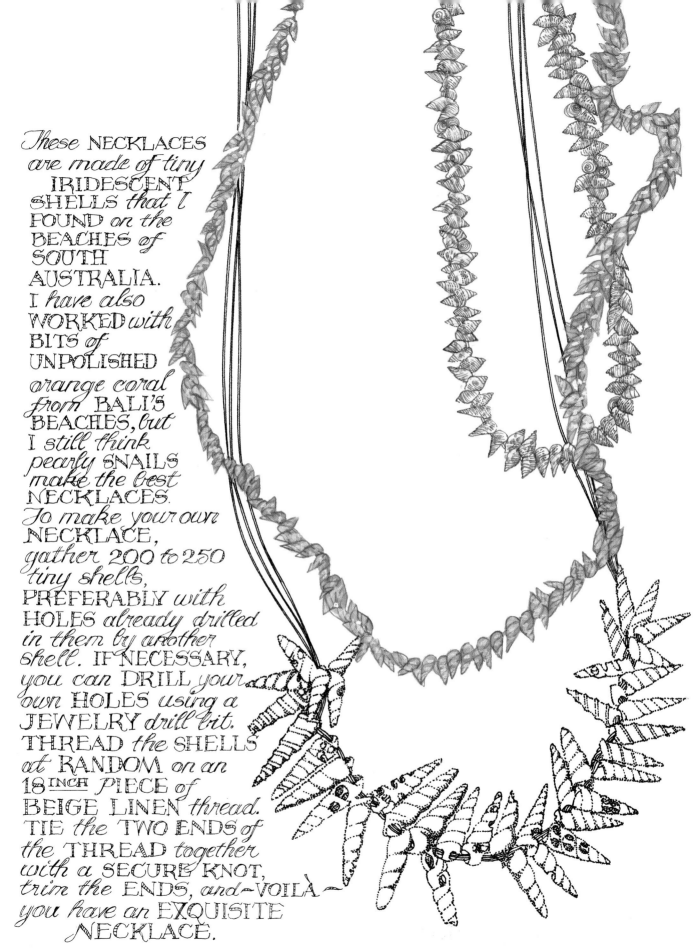

These NECKLACES are made of tiny IRIDESCENT SHELLS that I FOUND on the BEACHES of SOUTH AUSTRALIA. I have also WORKED with BITS of UNPOLISHED orange coral from BALI'S BEACHES, but I still think pearly SNAILS make the best NECKLACES. To make your own NECKLACE, gather 200 to 250 tiny shells, PREFERABLY with HOLES already drilled in them by another shell. IF NECESSARY, you can DRILL your own HOLES using a JEWELRY drill bit. THREAD the SHELLS at RANDOM on an 18 INCH PIECE of BEIGE LINEN thread. TIE the TWO ENDS of the THREAD together with a SECURE KNOT, trim the ENDS, and ~VOILÀ~ you have an EXQUISITE NECKLACE.

NERITES

SHOWN HERE IN TWO *of its many* COLOR VARIATIONS *is* NERITINA COMMUNIS. ALL NERITES *are* VEGETARIANS. THEY LIVE IN SWAMPS *as well as in the* SEA, AMONG ROCKS *and* CORALS.

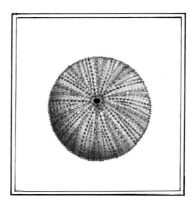

OLIVE SHELLS ·OLIVIDAE·
SHINY, HIGHLY DIVERSE, *and often* VERY COLORFUL, *the* OLIVE SHELL *is a* COLLECTORS' FAVORITE.

OYSTERS

THROUGHOUT the AGES there have BEEN MANY OYSTER CRAZES. The ROMAN EMPEROR TIBERIUS is said to have DOWNED a few HUNDRED OYSTERS BEFORE DINNER to WHET his APPETITE. IN THE 19th CENTURY, ABRAHAM LINCOLN had freshly PACKED EAST COAST OYSTERS SHIPPED all the way to ILLINOIS to ENTERTAIN his GUESTS. The LATEST FASHION is the SYDNEY rock oyster, which is a "MUST" for any VISITOR to AUSTRALIA.

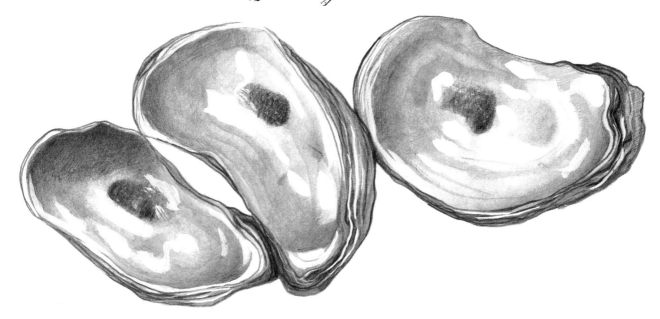

OYSTERS are best SERVED RAW. Place them on the HALF SHELL on a BED of ROCK SALT. SERVE with wedges of LEMON. FOR A WINTER BREAKFAST TREAT, try this RECIPE.

2 PINTS (about 16) OYSTERS, shucked, drained, liquor reserved
2 CUPS BREADCRUMBS seasoned with salt and pepper
1 STICK (8 tablespoons) BUTTER
4 SLICES of WHOLE-WHEAT TOAST

Toss the OYSTERS in the BREADCRUMBS. In a small pan MELT HALF the BUTTER and ADD the OYSTERS. Cook over low heat UNTIL the EDGES CURL. Place the OYSTERS on the toast, dividing them evenly. PUT the remaining BUTTER in the pan and gently HEAT the OYSTER LIQUOR, then POUR it over the OYSTERS on the TOAST. I like to add a shake of HOT SAUCE and serve with Bloody Marys. SERVES 4.

59

The
COCK'S COMB
OYSTER
Lopha cristagalli
from the
INDO~PACIFIC REGION.

BLACK~LIPPED
OYSTER
Pinctada margaritifera
FOUND *in the*
INDO~PACIFIC
REGION.

THIS OYSTER
and
Pinctada maxima
ARE *the* BEST SOURCES
of MOTHER~*of*~PEARL. THE SHELL
has been USED *by* NATIVES *of the*
PACIFIC *as a* RAZOR *and as a*
SHARP TOOL *for* CUTTING *or*
CHOPPING. IT HAS ALSO BEEN
USED *for* UTENSILS *such as*
the LARGE SERVING SPOON
SHOWN HERE *from the*
PITT RIVERS MUSEUM *in Oxford*
ENGLAND. AMONG *the other*
OBJECTS *on* DISPLAY *at*
this MUSEUM *are several*
HEADDRESSES *and*
BREAST PLATES
DECORATED *with this*
LARGE, IRIDESCENT SHELL.

IN EUROPE, *from the* 14TH
CENTURY ONWARD, BLACK~
LIPPED OYSTER SHELLS *were*
CARVED *and made into* PENDANTS
and also USED *as* INLAY *for* PANELS
and HOME ALTARS. FRANCISCAN MONKS CARVED
THEM *for use as* BAPTISMAL SPOONS, CROSSES,
and BOXES, *and* SOLD THEM *to* PILGRIMS *to the*
HOLY LAND. THE SHELLS *they* USED CAME *from*
the PERSIAN GULF REGION.

61

PAGODA SHELL

COLUMBARIUM PAGODA or COMMON PAGODA
found in deep water off the coast of Japan.

Aporrhais pespelicani

the
PELICAN'S
FOOT SHELL

IS AT HOME on the OCEAN FLOOR. IT IS SHOWN TURNED OVER HERE. *Normally,* ITS EXTENSIONS FORM a DOMELIKE FEEDING CHAMBER.

PEN SHELL

·Pinnidae·

THIS LARGE, FAN-SHAPED, FRAGILE SHELL LIVES PARTIALLY BURIED on the SANDY FLOOR of the OCEAN, ANCHORED to SEAWEED or ROCKS by its SILKY BYSSUS. This BYSSUS has been SPUN into a FABRIC by the PEOPLE of the MEDITERRANEAN BASIN since ancient times and may have been the GOLDEN FLEECE of GREEK MYTHOLOGY.

Pinna nobilis

64

PERIWINKLES _Littorinidae_

POACH 2 _pounds_ PERIWINKLES _in enough_ SALTED WATER _or_ BOUILLON STOCK _to cover them._ ADD _a branch of thyme, some black_ _peppercorns, or a_ FRESH RED CHILI PEPPER. BRING _to a_ BOIL, _then_ SIMMER _for about_ 5 _minutes over_ MEDIUM HEAT. _Remove_ _from_ HEAT _and_ LET _the_ PERIWINKLES COOL _in the_ BROTH. DRAIN _and_ SERVE _with_ HOMEMADE MAYONNAISSE. _Add a_ SQUEEZE _of_ LEMON _or make a dip_ _of_ FLAVORED VINEGAR.

Use toothpicks to _remove the snails_ _from their shells._

SERVES 4 AS AN APPETIZER.

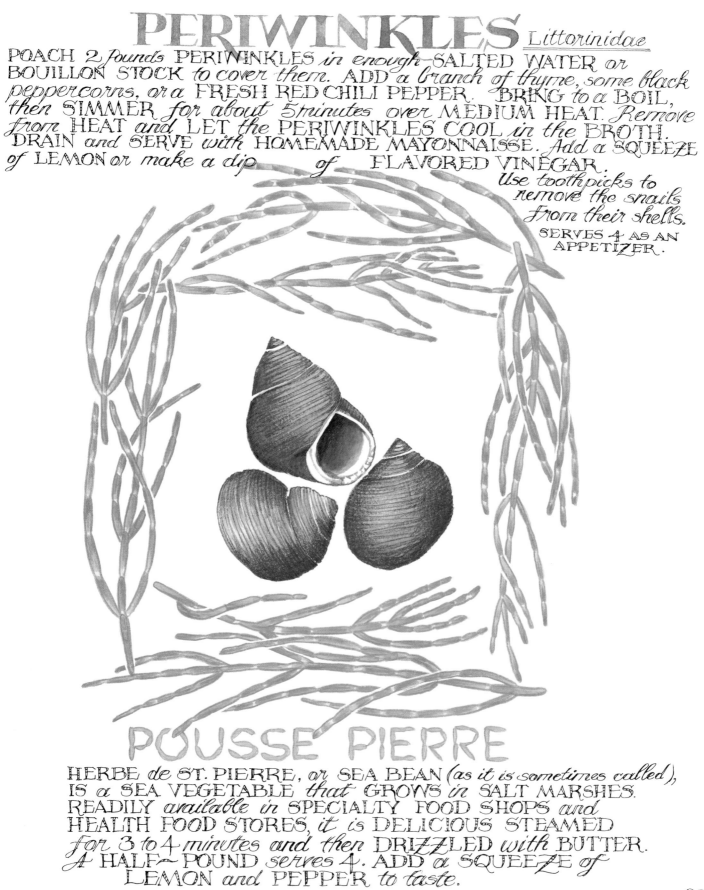

POUSSE PIERRE

HERBE _de_ ST. PIERRE, _or_ SEA BEAN (_as it is sometimes called_), IS _a_ SEA VEGETABLE _that_ GROWS _in_ SALT MARSHES. READILY _available in_ SPECIALTY FOOD SHOPS _and_ HEALTH FOOD STORES, _it is_ DELICIOUS STEAMED _for_ 3 _to_ 4 _minutes and then_ DRIZZLED _with_ BUTTER. A HALF~POUND _serves_ 4. ADD _a_ SQUEEZE _of_ LEMON _and_ PEPPER _to taste._

QUEEN
TEGULA
·Tegula regina·
CALIFORNIA

THIS THICK~SHELLED CLAM WAS MADE INTO
WAMPUM and TRADED by EAST COAST INDIANS,
often in the FORM of BELTS and NECKLACES.
The BEADS were STILL USED as CURRENCY
in the early 1800s.

QUAHOG

Mercenaria mercenaria

·STUFFED QUAHOGS·

2 DOZEN CLAMS
1 small ANCHOVY fillet
1 clove GARLIC
6 tablespoons BUTTER
juice of ½ LEMON

freshly ground BLACK PEPPER
and red pepper flakes to taste
3 cups ROCK SALT
6 sprigs PARSLEY, finely chopped
½ CUP BREADCRUMBS

STEAM the CLAMS just until they OPEN and set them
aside. PREHEAT OVEN to 350°F. CRUSH the
ANCHOVY and GARLIC in a MORTAR, then add the
BUTTER, lemon juice, black pepper, and red pepper
flakes to make a PASTE. PLACE the OPENED
HALF SHELLS with the CLAMS inside on a bed
of rock salt on an OVENPROOF DISH. COVER
each CLAM with a SPOONFUL of the PASTE.
MIX the PARSLEY and BREADCRUMBS and
SPRINKLE the mixture on top of EACH CLAM.
Bake for 10 minutes. SERVES 4 to 6.

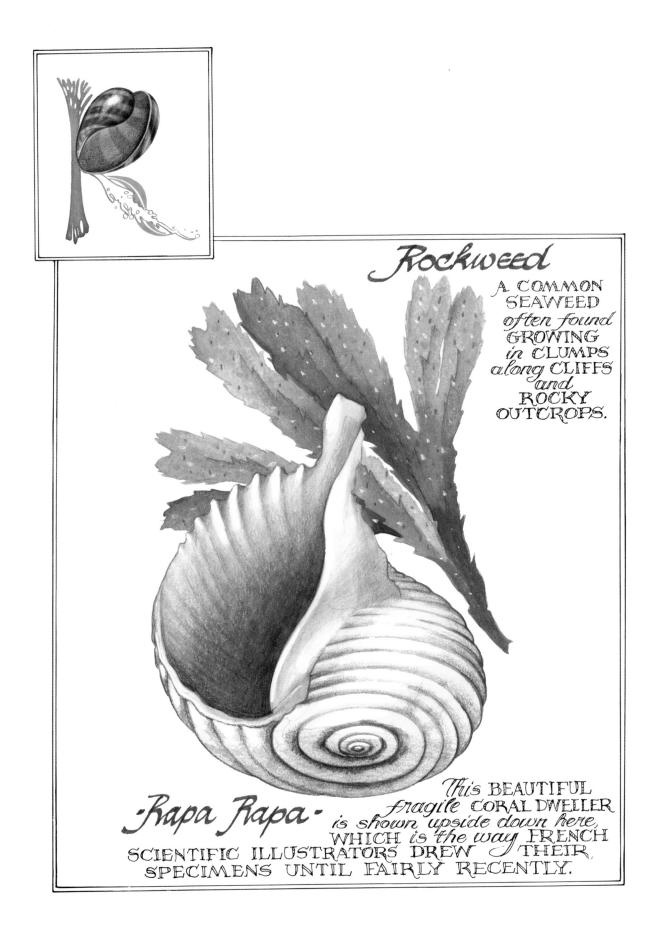

Rockweed

A COMMON SEAWEED *often found* GROWING *in* CLUMPS *along* CLIFFS *and* ROCKY OUTCROPS.

Rapa Rapa

This BEAUTIFUL *fragile* CORAL DWELLER *is shown upside down here,* WHICH *is the way* FRENCH SCIENTIFIC ILLUSTRATORS DREW THEIR SPECIMENS UNTIL FAIRLY RECENTLY.

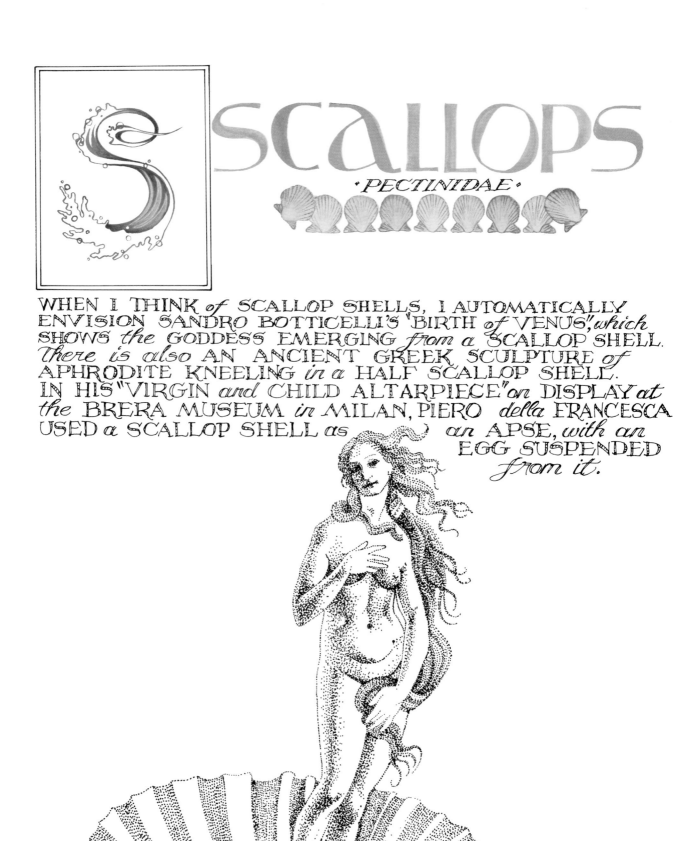

SCALLOPS

·PECTINIDAE·

WHEN I THINK of SCALLOP SHELLS, I AUTOMATICALLY ENVISION SANDRO BOTTICELLI'S "BIRTH of VENUS", which SHOWS the GODDESS EMERGING from a SCALLOP SHELL. There is also AN ANCIENT GREEK SCULPTURE of APHRODITE KNEELING in a HALF SCALLOP SHELL. IN HIS "VIRGIN and CHILD ALTARPIECE" on DISPLAY at the BRERA MUSEUM in MILAN, PIERO della FRANCESCA USED a SCALLOP SHELL as an APSE, with an EGG SUSPENDED from it.

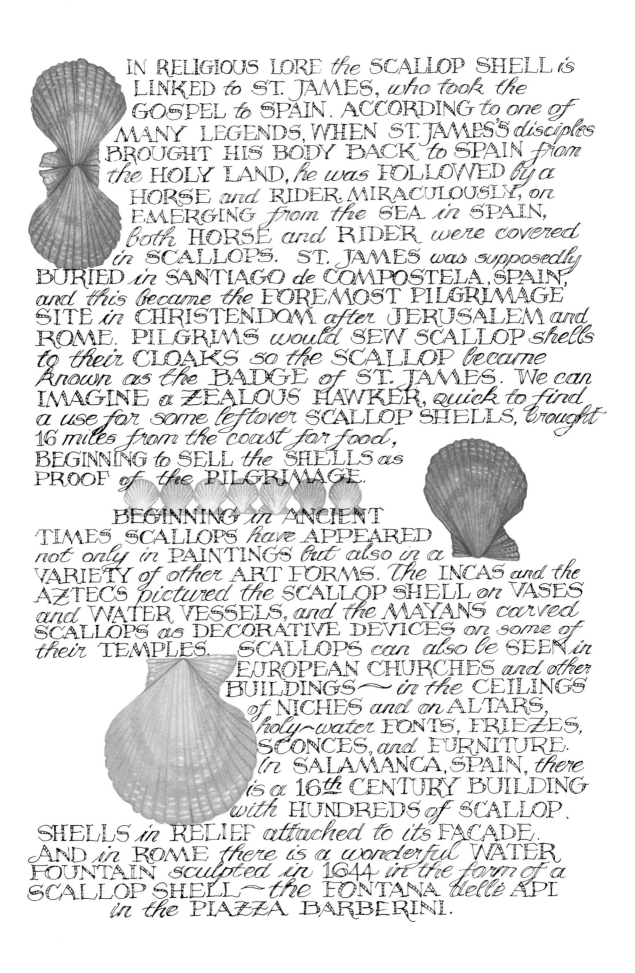

IN RELIGIOUS LORE the SCALLOP SHELL is LINKED to ST. JAMES, who took the GOSPEL to SPAIN. ACCORDING to one of MANY LEGENDS, WHEN ST. JAMES'S disciples BROUGHT HIS BODY BACK to SPAIN from the HOLY LAND, he was FOLLOWED by a HORSE and RIDER. MIRACULOUSLY, on EMERGING from the SEA in SPAIN, both HORSE and RIDER were covered in SCALLOPS. ST. JAMES was supposedly BURIED in SANTIAGO de COMPOSTELA, SPAIN, and this became the FOREMOST PILGRIMAGE SITE in CHRISTENDOM after JERUSALEM and ROME. PILGRIMS would SEW SCALLOP shells to their CLOAKS so the SCALLOP became known as the BADGE of ST. JAMES. We can IMAGINE a ZEALOUS HAWKER, quick to find a use for some leftover SCALLOP SHELLS, brought 16 miles from the coast for food, BEGINNING to SELL the SHELLS as PROOF of the PILGRIMAGE.

BEGINNING in ANCIENT TIMES SCALLOPS have APPEARED not only in PAINTINGS but also in a VARIETY of other ART FORMS. The INCAS and the AZTECS pictured the SCALLOP SHELL on VASES and WATER VESSELS, and the MAYANS carved SCALLOPS as DECORATIVE DEVICES on some of their TEMPLES. SCALLOPS can also be SEEN in EUROPEAN CHURCHES and other BUILDINGS ~ in the CEILINGS of NICHES and on ALTARS, holy~water FONTS, FRIEZES, SCONCES, and FURNITURE. In SALAMANCA, SPAIN, there is a 16th CENTURY BUILDING with HUNDREDS of SCALLOP. SHELLS in RELIEF attached to its FACADE. AND in ROME there is a wonderful WATER FOUNTAIN sculpted in 1644 in the form of a SCALLOP SHELL ~ the FONTANA delle API in the PIAZZA BARBERINI.

GINGERED Scallops

1 POUND
BAY or SEA SCALLOPS
1 inch piece of GINGER ROOT,
Peeled and finely chopped
3 tablespoons BUTTER
JUICE of ½ LEMON
⅛ teaspoon CAYENNE PEPPER
SALT and freshly ground BLACK PEPPER to taste
A few sprigs of CORIANDER LEAVES, chopped

RINSE the SCALLOPS AND PAT DRY.
SAUTÉ the GINGER in the BUTTER for 2 mins.
over a LOW HEAT. ADD the SCALLOPS and
CONTINUE COOKING, stirring the
INGREDIENTS TOGETHER, for ANOTHER
2 minutes. ADD the LEMON JUICE,
CAYENNE, SALT, and BLACK PEPPER.
Do not overcook.
SERVE the SCALLOPS
and THEIR JUICE
over BASMATI RICE.
Sprinkle with chopped
CORIANDER.

SERVES 4.

Strawberry Top Shell
VASE

·CLANCULUS·
puniceus

An INEXPENSIVE CERAMIC VASE can be transformed into an EXOTIC JARDINIERE by a covering of SNAIL SHELLS like the strawberry top shells I'VE USED HERE. GATHER enough SHELLS to COVER a vase of YOUR CHOICE. Start with the TOP HALF of the VASE. Smooth on a LAYER of TILE CEMENT, which is available in a variety of colors from a hardware store. THEN place the SHELLS in neat ROWS moving from the RIM DOWN. WHEN YOU REACH the CENTER, apply CEMENT to the LOWER HALF and CONTINUE attaching SHELLS until you REACH the bottom. Don't WORRY if YOUR LAST ROW isn't completely EVEN — it won't be noticeable on the bottom. NOW LET the VASE DRY for 24 hrs. so the SHELLS are firmly CEMENTED in PLACE.

SLIT SHELL

·Pleurotomaria·

ALTHOUGH there are many FOSSILS of SLIT SHELLS from millions of years ago, today it is a rarity, found only in very DEEP WATERS. It gets its NAME *from* a wide SLIT *in its bottom* WHORL. The ANIMAL *uses this* SLIT *to* EXPEL *its waste.*

Sargasso Seaweed·

IN the NORTH ATLANTIC, *near* BERMUDA, *there is a* HUGE AREA *of* RELATIVELY STILL WATER *filled with* FLOATING *brown* SEAWEED *of the genus* SARGASSUM. *This* AREA *is* KNOWN *as the* SARGASSO SEA, *and many a wary* CAPTAIN *has* REFUSED *to* VENTURE *through it.*

STARFISH

Asteroidea

These DECEPTIVELY beautiful STARFISH are among the most VORACIOUS CARNIVORES to SCOUR the OCEAN FLOOR. They are NOT truly shellfish, although most SHELL collections INCLUDE a FEW. AMONG my SHELLS, I HAVE a tiny STARFISH that I found in a BOUILLABAISSE in a LOCAL FRENCH RESTAURANT.

STARFISH VARY greatly in COLOR, SIZE, and shape. ONE SPIDERY STARFISH from the GULF of MEXICO measures 4 to 5 FEET from TENTACLE to TENTACLE. Another FORMIDABLE CREATURE is the CROWN~of~THORNS STARFISH, which has frightening ARMORLIKE SPIKES on top. This STARFISH was INTRODUCED to the GREAT BARRIER REEF in Australia IN ORDER to kill off CERTAIN UNWANTED SEA CREATURES, but it has TURNED OUT to be an EVEN BIGGER PROBLEM, devouring the CORALS of the REEF ITSELF.

SHELLFISH STEW with LEEK and SEAWEED "SPAGHETTI"

for the stock:

1 LARGE ONION, *chopped*

2 LEEKS, *tender green and white parts, roughly chopped*

1/2 HEAD FENNEL, *or* 1 *teaspoon* FENNEL SEEDS

8 STALKS CELERY HEART *with* LEAVES, *chopped*

1/3 CUP OLIVE OIL

3/4 BOTTLE (1 LITER) WHITE WINE

2 CUPS WATER

4 POUNDS *non-oily* FISH FRAMES *and* HEADS

4 POUNDS TOMATOES, *quartered*

4 CLOVES GARLIC

1 BOUQUET GARNI

1/4 *teaspoon* SAFFRON THREADS

ZEST *of* 1 ORANGE

JUICE *of* 1 LEMON

1/2 *teaspoon* SALT

1/4 *teaspoon ground* BLACK PEPPER

1/8 *teaspoon* HOT PEPPER FLAKES

To prepare the Stock:
MAKE STOCK A DAY AHEAD.
IN a LARGE, HEAVY SAUCEPAN soften the ONION,
LEEKS, FENNEL, and CELERY in the OIL~ about 5
minutes. ADD the WINE, WATER, FISH, TOMATOES,
and other INGREDIENTS, COVER, bring to a boil,
and then SIMMER for ½ hour. STRAIN the STOCK
and PRESS it through a MESH COLANDER with
the BACK of a wooden spoon. LET IT COOL.
Refrigerate for 24 hours.

For the Stew:
2 LEEKS, tender green and white parts, finely sliced
2 tablespoons OLIVE OIL
1 Pound MUSSELS
1 Pound MEDIUM SHRIMP, unpeeled
1 Pound QUAHOGS or LITTLENECK CLAMS
1 Pound SEA SCALLOPS
2 Sheets NORI SEAWEED, folded and cut
   into strands with kitchen scissors

To prepare the Stew:
IN A LARGE, HEAVY SAUCEPAN, soften the LEEKS
in OIL~ about 5 minutes. ADD the STOCK and
bring to a BOIL, then SIMMER. ADD the MUSSELS,
SHRIMP, and CLAMS, followed by the SCALLOPS.
Then toss in the SEAWEED STRANDS.
Simmer 2 minutes more. ADJUST the SEASONING,
adding SALT and PEPPER to taste. LADLE out
PORTIONS of SHELLFISH and "SPAGHETTI" with
the STOCK into SOUP BOWLS. Put an EXTRA
BOWL on the table for the EMPTY SHELLS.
SERVE with CRUSTY BREAD and a GREEN SALAD.
                 SERVES 6 to 8.

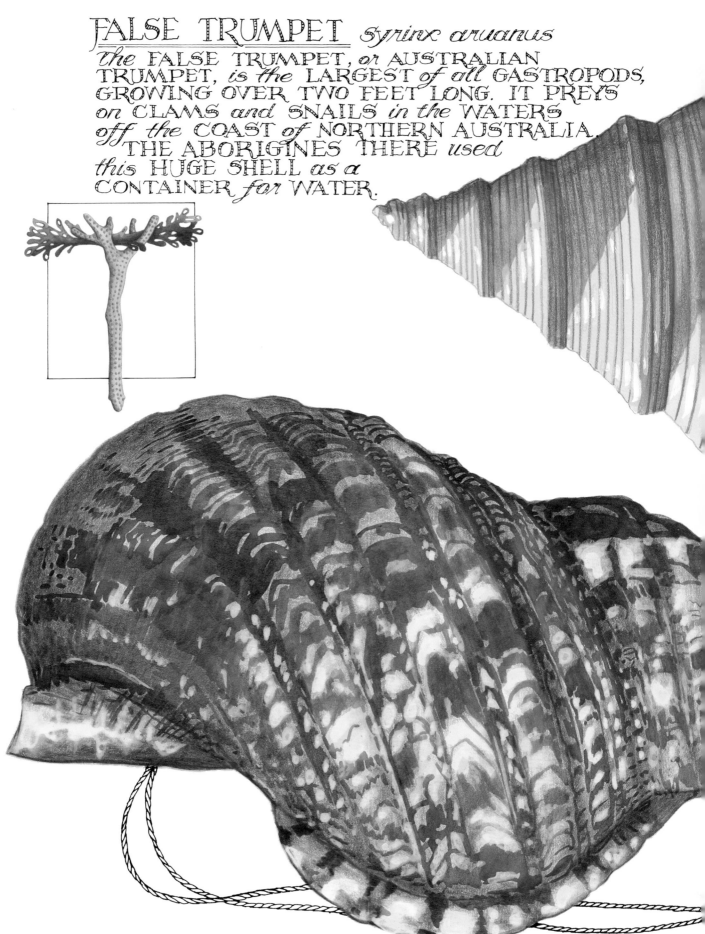

FALSE TRUMPET *Syrinx aruanus*

the FALSE TRUMPET, or AUSTRALIAN TRUMPET, is the LARGEST of all GASTROPODS, GROWING OVER TWO FEET LONG. IT PREYS on CLAMS and SNAILS in the WATERS off the COAST of NORTHERN AUSTRALIA. THE ABORIGINES THERE used this HUGE SHELL as a CONTAINER for WATER.

TRITON SHELL
Cymatiidae

BY CUTTING off the SPIRE and DRILLING a HOLE in the BULBOUS PART of the TRITON SHELL, EARLY PEOPLES TURNED this SHELL into a TRUMPET. LATER, SOME of these "TRUMPETS" were fitted with MOUTHPIECES and REEDS, as well as CARRYING THONGS. IN FACT, the SHELL is often called "TRITON'S TRUMPET" because TRITON, the son of the GREEK SEA GOD POSEIDON, supposedly BLEW a SHELL to CALL the DEITIES TOGETHER. TRITON SHELLS are part of the MYTHOLOGY and FOLKLORE of NOT ONLY the MEDITERRANEAN but also the PACIFIC. These CARNIVORES can grow to 16 inches. THEY LIVE in and around CORAL REEFS, where they FEED ON STARFISH.

79

TUN·Shells

THESE LARGE, FRAGILE~LOOKING, SCULPTURED CARNIVORES *feed mainly* on SEA URCHINS *and small* CRUSTACEANS *that* LIVE *in* TROPICAL WATERS.

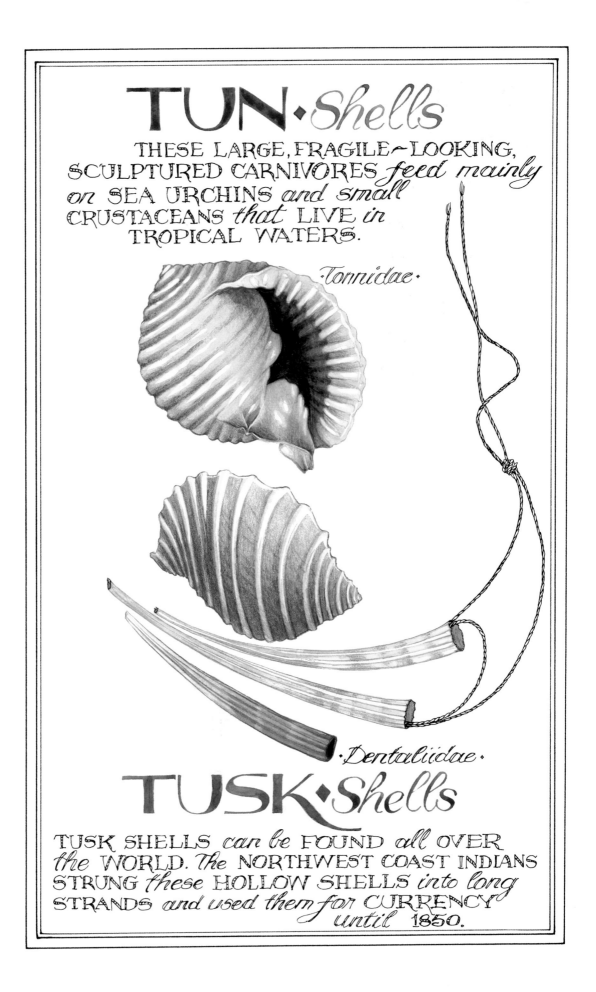

Tonnidae·

·Dentaliidae·

TUSK·Shells

TUSK SHELLS *can be* FOUND *all* OVER *the* WORLD. *The* NORTHWEST COAST INDIANS STRUNG *these* HOLLOW SHELLS *into long* STRANDS *and used them for* CURRENCY *until* 1850.

TURRIDS

·Turridae·

The JAPANESE TURRID SHELL SEEMS to REFLECT the ARCHITECTURE of the ORIENT. OTHER MEMBERS of this LARGE, ANCIENT FAMILY have a VENOMOUS STING, WHICH they USE for DEFENSE or to CAPTURE PREY.

Green TURBAN

Turbo marmoratus

THIS LUSH, DARK GREEN, HEAVY SHELL *is found in the* TROPICAL WATERS *of the* EAST INDIES *and along the* COAST *of* AUSTRALIA. IT *has a* WONDERFUL, WIDE PEARLY APERTURE. IF *the* SHELL'S OUTER LAYER *is* REMOVED, *the* LAYERS UNDERNEATH *give off an* IRIDESCENT GLOW~ *so it is* OFTEN *used for* INLAYS *and* JEWELRY.

TOP SHELLS

·Trochidae·

When the EUROPEANS discovered HUGE BEDS of TOP SHELLS off the COASTS of AUSTRALIA, NEW ZEALAND, and the NEARBY PACIFIC ISLANDS, they gathered ALMOST ALL of these SHELLS, using them MOSTLY to make BUTTONS. WITH the invention of PLASTIC BUTTONS, the DECLINE of these BEAUTIFUL SHELLS was REVERSED. These SHELLS are GRADUALLY REESTABLISHING THEMSELVES, BUT THEY are "SLOW GROWERS"— IT TAKES THEM SIX YEARS to REACH MATURITY.

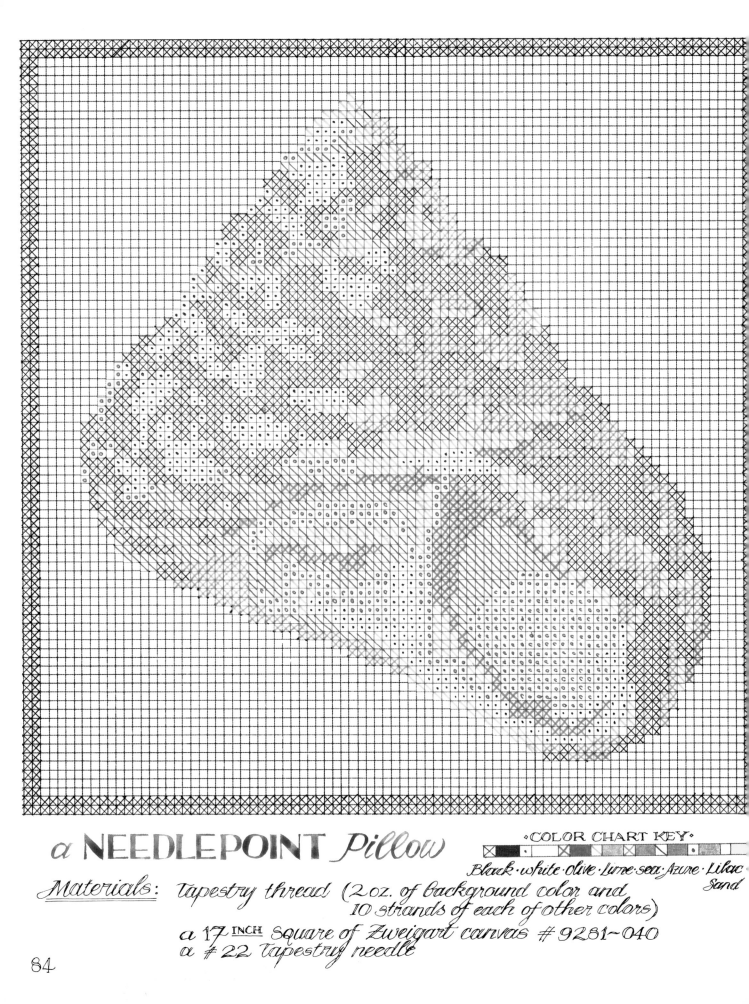

a **NEEDLEPOINT** *Pillow*

<u>*Materials*</u>: *Tapestry thread (2 oz. of background color and 10 strands of each of other colors)*
    a 17^{INCH} *square of Zweigart canvas #9281~040*
    a #22 Tapestry needle

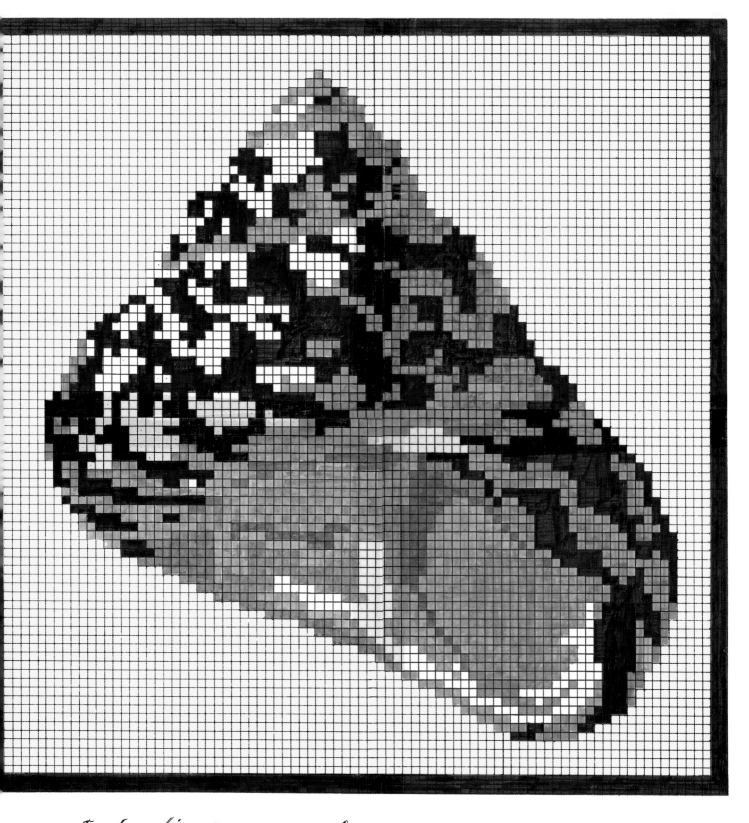

UMBONIINAE

Umbonium giganteum

THESE SHINY, *rather flat,* INCH~LONG SHELLS *are commonly called* BUTTON SHELLS, *and they belong to the* SAME FAMILY *as* TOP SHELLS. LARGE QUANTITIES *of these* SHELLS, *in varied patterns,* CAN BE FOUND *in the* MUDDY BAYS *of* SOUTHEAST ASIA.

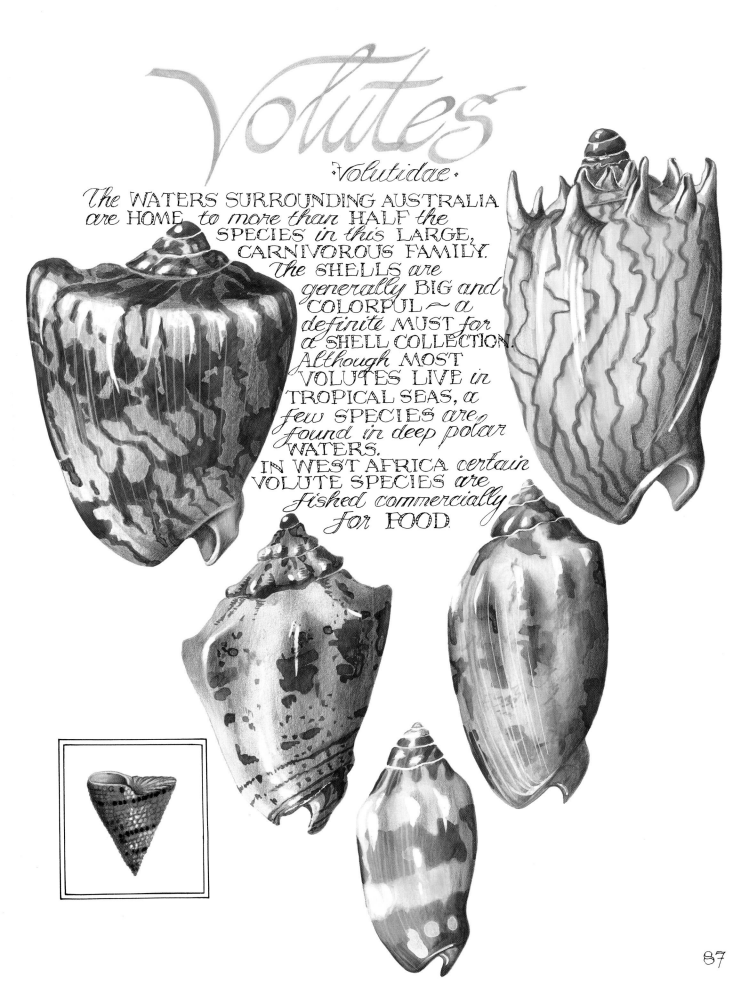

Volutes

· Volutidae ·

The WATERS SURROUNDING AUSTRALIA are HOME to more than HALF the SPECIES in this LARGE, CARNIVOROUS FAMILY. The SHELLS are generally BIG and COLORFUL ~ a definite MUST for a SHELL COLLECTION. Although MOST VOLUTES LIVE in TROPICAL SEAS, a few SPECIES are found in deep polar WATERS. IN WEST AFRICA certain VOLUTE SPECIES are fished commercially for FOOD.

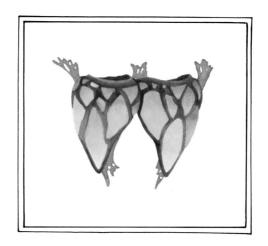

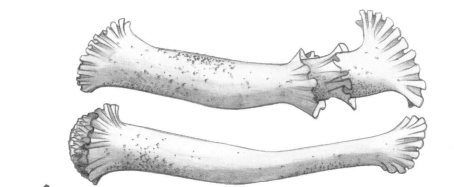

The WATERING POT Clam

Penicillus penis

This UNUSUAL SHELL *begins life as a* NORMAL
BIVALVE BUT GROWS *into a* LONG TUBULAR
SHAPE. IT LIVES PARTIALLY BURIED *in the*
OCEAN FLOOR. ITS BASE, *which is* BURIED,
RESEMBLES *a* SUNFLOWER.

WORMSHELLS

Vermiculariinae, Turritellidae, Siliquariidae

These MOLLUSKS almost always
LIVE in SPONGES in WARM WATERS
all over the WORLD. THEY START
OUT with a SMALL SNAIL~LIKE
form but DEVELOP an INDIVIDUAL
SHAPE by TWISTING RANDOMLY
around the SPONGE.

WENTLETRAPS

EPITONIIDAE

The Magnificent Wentletrap

·AMAEA MAGNIFICA·

The MAGNIFICENT WENTLETRAP is one of the LARGEST WENTLETRAPS, GROWING UP TO 5 INCHES LONG. This RARE SHELL is IDENTIFIABLE by its HORIZONTAL and VERTICAL RIBS. Because it LIVES in VERY DEEP WATERS, SCIENTISTS have not BEEN ABLE TO OBSERVE its HABITS and it REMAINS QUITE mysterious.

Precious Wentletrap

Epitonium scalare

STORMS *have* RECENTLY *beached* THOUSANDS *of these* ONCE RARE *shells* ALONG *the* COASTS *of* AUSTRALIA. ABOUT 200 YEARS AGO *they were considered as* PRECIOUS *as* GOLD *or* JEWELS, *and* SOME *industrious artisans from* CHINA *supposedly used* RICE PASTE *to make* EXACT REPLICAS *of these* SHELLS. LIVE WENTLETRAPS *feed on* SEA ANEMONES, CORALS, JELLYFISH, *and other small* ANIMALS, *sometimes* DEVOURING *the whole* ANIMAL.

Tropical Whelks

Babylonia zelandica

• BUCCINIDAE •

these pretty SHELLS *belong to a* LARGE FAMILY, *but the* cold~water SPECIES *are not as colorful as the* TROPICAL ONES. WHELKS ARE GENERALLY CARNIVORES. *they are* GATHERED *for* FOOD *in parts of* ASIA.

91

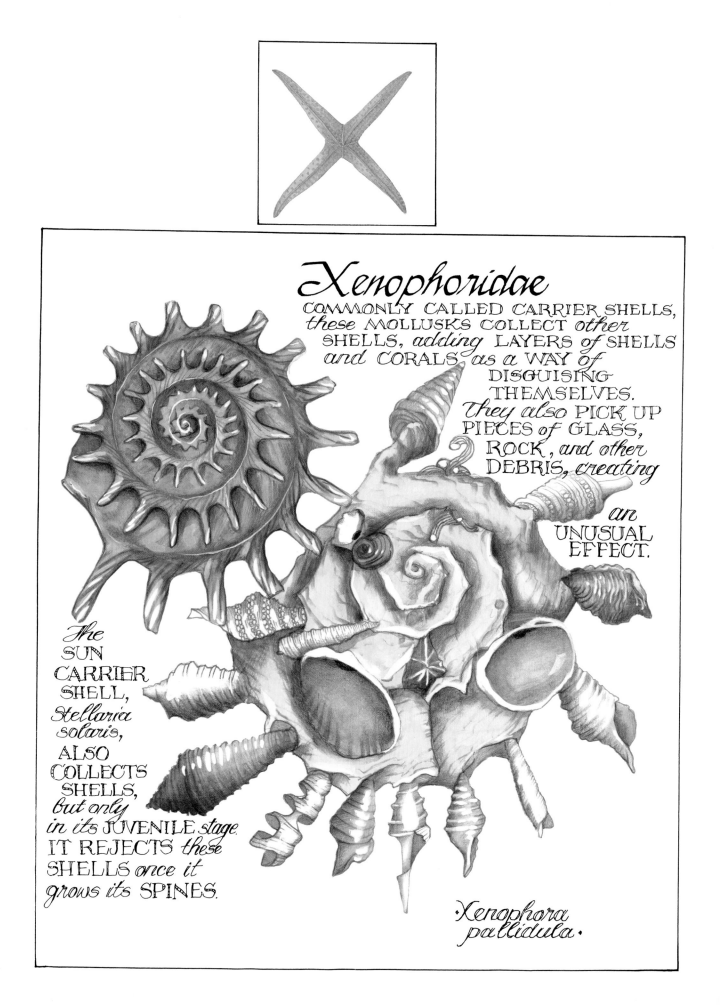

Xenophoridae

COMMONLY CALLED CARRIER SHELLS, these MOLLUSKS COLLECT other SHELLS, adding LAYERS of SHELLS and CORALS as a WAY of DISGUISING THEMSELVES. They also PICK UP PIECES of GLASS, ROCK, and other DEBRIS, creating an UNUSUAL EFFECT.

The SUN CARRIER SHELL, Stellaria solaris, ALSO COLLECTS SHELLS, but only in its JUVENILE stage. IT REJECTS these SHELLS once it grows its SPINES.

Xenophora pallidula.

YELLOW DRUPE

Drupa grossularia

THIS INCH~LONG, BRIGHTLY COLORED SHELL LIVES *in the* CORAL REEFS *of the* INDIAN *and* PACIFIC OCEANS.

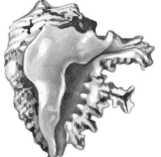

YELLOW UMBRELLA

Umbraculum pictum

A BRIGHT, BRITTLE ROCK~POOL DWELLER *this* SHELL *is* USUALLY CAMOUFLAGED *by* TINY CRUSTACEANS *or* ALGAE.

WAGNER'S ZAPLAGIUS
Zaplagius navicula
This largely COASTAL SNAIL
is mostly found SOUTH of
the EQUATOR.

ZIGZAG VENUS
*Lioconcha
castrensis*
This CREATURE LIVES
on CORAL REEFS
from the RED SEA
to the mid-
Pacific Region.

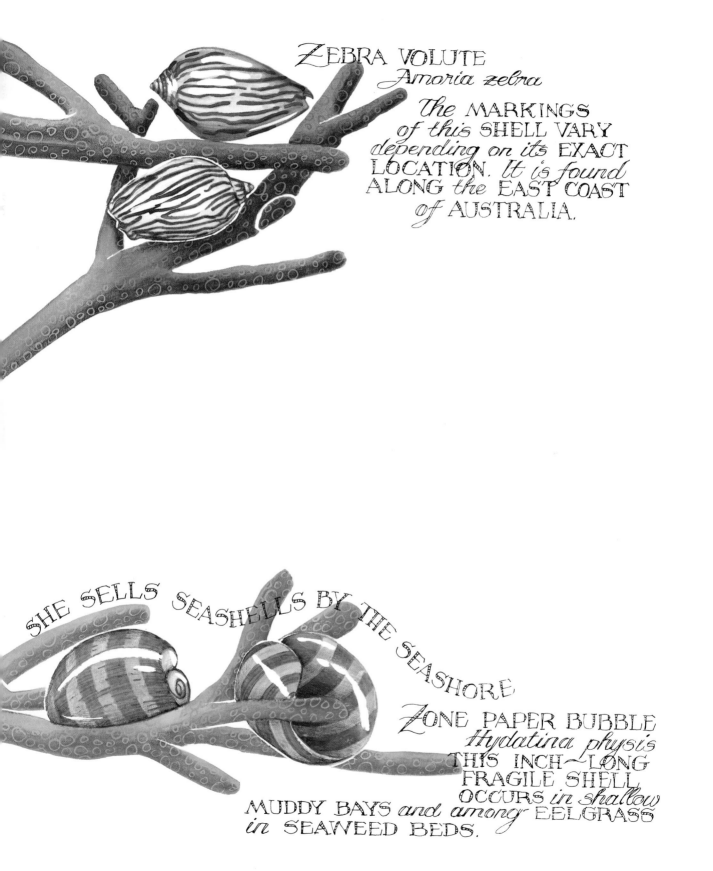

ZEBRA VOLUTE
Amoria zebra

The MARKINGS of this SHELL VARY depending on its EXACT LOCATION. *It is found* ALONG the EAST COAST *of* AUSTRALIA.

SHE SELLS SEASHELLS BY THE SEASHORE

ZONE PAPER BUBBLE
Hydatina physis
THIS INCH~LONG FRAGILE SHELL OCCURS *in shallow* MUDDY BAYS *and among* EELGRASS *in* SEAWEED BEDS.

INDEX

METRIC EQUIVALENTS

1 TEASPOON : 5 milliliters or 5 grams
1 TABLESPOON : 15 milliliters
1 CUP : 237 milliliters
1 POUND (16 oz.) : 454 grams
1 INCH : 2.54 centimeters
1 FOOT : 30.48 centimeters